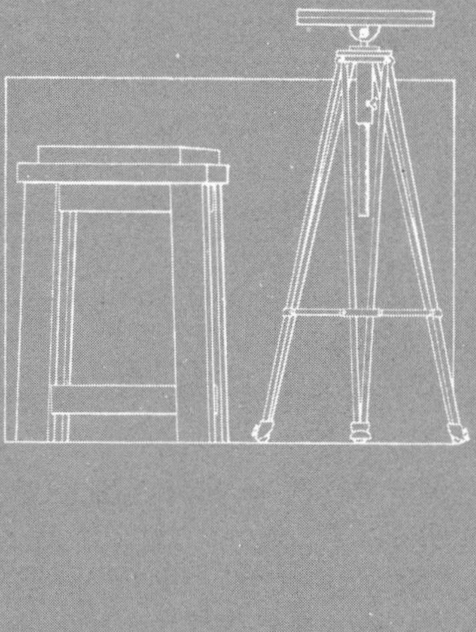

# taking up sculpture

**Taplinger's Teach-Yourself-Crafts Series**

Taking Up Drawing and Painting
Taking Up Sculpture
Scale Models in Balsa

Sean Mullaney

# taking up sculpture



TAPLINGER PUBLISHING COMPANY / NEW YORK

First published in the United States in 1973 by
TAPLINGER PUBLISHING CO., INC.
New York, New York



Library of Congress Catalog Card Number: 72-2201

ISBN 0-8008-7544-3

# Contents

**Note to American Readers**

The following terms may be unfamiliar to some American readers and are accordingly clarified to facilitate the use of this book:

Scrim——light coarse cotton fabric
Perspex——lucite

# Acknowledgements

I would like to express my thanks and appreciation first to my wife for her patient assistance and constant encouragement. To all my teachers and students who have taught me so much. To the artists who have made their works available to me and to Kate Ohly, Lotte Reiniger, Laura Gilbert and Hussein Abbo who have lent pieces from their collections. To E. Jackson for the photograph of 'Scorpio Major' and to E. J. Simmons for his photographs of 'Portrait' by Fay Simmons and my 'Fertility Figure'.

Sean Mullaney
The Abbey Art Centre

# Illustrations

1

# The creative process

All children naturally enjoy and learn from the creative manipulation of material. In primitive societies this satisfaction plays an important part throughout the whole of a person's life. Today unfortunately the impersonal pressures of our society make it difficult for us to find a necessary outlet for this creativity. Many people who would benefit from the increased awareness and the satisfactions of a developing craftsmanship which are the rewards of sculpture are dissuaded by the popular though misleading idea of the artist manfully chipping away at a large block of marble. In fact carving is only one of the many branches of this art and I hope that a knowledge of the variety of possible techniques will open up this immensely satisfying art form to a greater number of potential sculptors. Once a person decides to take up sculpture, acquiring the necessary craftsmanship is largely a matter of patience and practice. On the creative side there can never be any hard and fast rules, but in this chapter I hope to provide a foundation on which a personal method of working can be built. If there is a genuine desire for both self-development and self-expression the creative process can be divided into three separate but interrelated stages: stimulus, information and communication.

First stimulus: as sensitive people we respond to the

stimulus of everyday experiences with a variety of emotions such as joy, sorrow, anger and so on.

Unfortunately, due to the stress of modern life, these responses can become automatic and no longer move us deeply. In order to develop as artists we must reverse this process and look at things in the way we did as young children, so that roses are not automatically beautiful and cabbages are not automatically ugly. Once we start to do this it will not only help us to be better artists but we will also be rewarded by a much greater awareness and enjoyment of our surroundings. We will no longer be dependent on the occasional or the dramatic to stimulate us.

The second stage in the creative process is concerned with information. By this I mean the questioning in depth of the situations to which we respond, so that we clearly understand both their nature and their form. It is important for the sculptor to be able to extract from the wealth of stimulation available that which can be usefully used as a basis for his sculpture. I would advise the reader to avoid situations where the content is imprecise; for example, it is impossible to model the smell of onions and there could be much heart-break or self-deception in the attempt. It is argued by some people that they could provide a visual equivalent for this sort of stimulus but I feel that as we are surrounded by genuine visual three-dimensional situations of incredible interest and variety, it would be somewhat perverse to ignore them in order to pursue such vague ideas.

When we are sure that our stimulation is genuine and that we have gathered as much information about it as we can, we come to the third stage which is the one concerned with communication. It is at this stage that we begin to make decisions about the final form that the sculpture will take. As we make our decisions about the material, method and size, etc. we must remember that our intention is to communicate the information that we now have, about our original stimulation, so that our experience can be shared. In general, I have found that the simplest statement is usually the most effective, but I am afraid that it is also the most difficult to achieve. To do this one must consider all the possibilities inherent in a situation in order to eliminate the unimportant while retaining the essentials.

I would now like to develop the method I have outlined in relation to making a sculpture derived from a pebble picked up on a beach. I have chosen this particular example because it shows that it is possible to make a sculpture based on something that at one time or another most people will have collected, or at least seen and handled. My workshop is full of bric-à-brac that I have collected on the basis that one day it might be useful, including a selection of pebbles picked up at different times from various beaches. I would use as a starting point for my sculpture the fact that out of the millions of pebbles which I could have chosen, I took the trouble to bring these particular ones home; consequently they must have something special about them that interested me at the time. I try to recreate the original situation in miniature, by selecting from the hundred or so pebbles that I possess, the one which appeals to me the most. For me the sculpture stage proper begins when I look at the pebble I have chosen, and ask myself, Why? I must now examine it very carefully, for a considerable length of time, because it will be upon the decisions that I now take that I will base the constructive criticisms which will guide me through the whole time I am working on the sculpture. If I did not clearly know what it was that excited me about the pebble, how could I decide how well or how badly I was communicating this excitement? I also know that sculpture, by its nature, is a lengthy process and I would want to make sure that I am sufficiently interested in the shape of the pebble to be able to retain that excitement through to the end. I also want to be clear at this stage whether or not my interest in the pebble is a genuine response to its actual shape or if perhaps it interests me because it resembles something else, for example a bird's egg or a more precious stone. I must make certain at this stage of the foundation on which I am going to build. It is quite possible that at a later stage I might wish to incorporate other ideas, but I believe it to be important to keep the original concept clearly in mind throughout the work, otherwise I might go on for ever hopefully adding a piece here, taking a piece off there – in effect just doodling on a large scale.

On examination of my pebble I find that the one I have chosen does not consciously remind me of anything else and that I do continue to respond to its actual shape. In form it is round and fat at one end, tapering away to a sharp point at the other. I suppose that I respond immediately to this contrast in shape because it is usual to respond to contrast. If you remember how much more pleasant it is to be warm indoors if a cold wind is howling outside, you will realize that our awareness of any situation is made much more intense if we are also aware of its opposite. In fact I would go further and claim that it is impossible to know a situation if we do not also know its opposite. It is only when we look at the stationary landscape from a train window that we become aware of the speed at which we are travelling.

Once I am reassured that my interest in the pebble is on a sound basis, I can study its form in more detail, looking for similar if less immediately obvious characteristics. On doing this I find that this element of contrast occurs again and again, in varying degrees, between areas which are flat and areas which are curved. I find that there is also contrast between different parts of the surface, which is worn smooth in some places but pitted and rough in others. It is quite possible that the pebble would have been wet when I first picked it up on the beach and so it would be a good idea at this stage, to see if wetting it again might improve its appearance. The resultant shiny surface shows up more clearly the points I had already noticed, and reveals even more subtle qualities. I may decide at this stage that the finished sculpture should have a polished surface. A further characteristic of the pebble which excites me is that, although all these different qualities are playing against each other, the pebble, like most natural forms, retains an amazing feeling of balance and unity. I would hope to get this quality into my sculpture because, although imbalance can be dramatic, I feel that in something as permanent as sculpture, balance is a quality that we can continue to enjoy over a long period of time.

I find in making this close examination of the pebble that my original enthusiasm has returned and that I can enjoy spending a long time just holding it and looking at it from different positions and angles. From doing this I learn two more things. First, that in one position more than in any other the qualities that I admire are more readily apparent. This helps me to make a decision about the final composition of the sculpture. I also notice another very interesting characteristic: I find that when I hold the pebble at eye level and view it against a distant background, it appears to change in size, and become more exciting because of its isolation. I then realize that, as far as my sculpture is concerned, the actual size of the pebble is not important and that I can with advantage make my sculpture much larger. This is a very necessary point to emphasize, because in making sculpture we should not merely be copying from nature, but making a selection of the qualities we feel to be the most important. We should not hesitate to change and simplify if this will enable us to attain our goal of communication more clearly.

I now feel that I have sufficient knowledge of my source to start making the actual sculpture, or at least to start some small exploratory models, which we usually call *maquettes*.

## Two exercises in awareness and observation

We have seen how the making of a sculpture involves the deliberate use of our visual senses. It is important that we develop this awareness, not only when we are making a sculpture, but as often as we possibly can. For this reason I would now like to give the details of two exercises. The first is designed to increase one's awareness of the subtleties of form; the second is concerned with observation and with making definite decisions.

The first exercise involves the use of any two similar objects. Fruit is generally an ideal choice here, and I would like to illustrate what is involved by using two oranges for my example. If they were bought at the same price they will, at first glance, be quite indistinguishable from each other. But if we examine them carefully we will see that although they are both obviously oranges they are not exactly the same shape. The exercise now falls into two parts. First, we must try to decide what it is they have in common – what it is that makes them both recognizable as oranges. In fact, what we are trying to do is to isolate the essential *orangeness* of all oranges. The second part of the exercise comes when we put the oranges side by side and compare them, this time trying to isolate their individual characteristics. It can help one's concentration to draw or to make small models of the objects, but what is most important is to get into the habit of this way of looking at things during the course of our everyday life. We have already discussed the importance of contrast, and this exercise with the oranges should make us aware of the contrast that exists between what they have in common and their actual individualities. This of course applies to most natural phenomena, including ourselves. Most people have two eyes, a nose and a mouth, which are in roughly the same place, are more or less the same shape, and perform the same functions for everybody. The world is full of people who look like people, trees that look like trees, birds that look like birds, but each of them has a separate subtle individual identity. A constant awareness of this is the source of sensitivity.

The second exercise is designed to train the eye and also to make one more aware of the nature of space and volume. It can be performed anywhere and at any time when the mind is not too preoccupied by other considerations. The exercise consists of taking any two dissimilar objects which are in close proximity to each other, and comparing them together. It could, for example, be a telephone kiosk and a post box or a teapot and a milk bottle. Let us call one object A and the other B. The exercise starts by making the most obvious comparisons first: for example, is A larger than B? If the answer is yes, by roughly how much? Is it twice as big or only one and a half times as big? Is it longer, narrower or wider? If we were to put B into A would it stick out anywhere? And so on, gradually asking ourselves more complex questions. This use of the comparative method to arrive at decisions can be quite enjoyable, almost a game, but it is also invaluable training.

## The work of other artists

The final part of this chapter is concerned with the relationship between the would-be sculptor and the work of other artists. There are some genuine artists who are known as 'primitives', which is not a term of abuse but means that their work is not influenced by the techniques or discoveries of other artists, or by the history of art. Their work often has great charm and is much admired, particularly at a time when the work of most professional artists makes considerable demands on the part of the viewer. However, it is exceedingly difficult in the normal environment of the twentieth century to remain immune from some sort of visual influence, especially from the all-pervasive advertising media, which is visually very sophisticated. Once you become aware of these influences it is possible to select those which will be of the greatest benefit to you, but having been influenced in this way you cannot really consider yourself to be working in the 'primitive' manner because whatever you do is no longer purely spontaneous activity. This means that you have, in however humble a position, joined the mainstream of art which flows from the first cave paintings made so many thousands of years ago.

This may sound somewhat overawing, but if you remember that art, at least in the creative sense, is not competitive, you should not be too discouraged. Everything that people create is important, nor does it have to be great art to give pleasure. All genuine creative effort makes a valuable contribution to the continuation of true civilization. The art galleries and museums which contain some of the most important art treasures of the world are available to you and it is up to you to take advantage of them.

In this respect, I think that it is very important for a person to develop his own individual taste by calling upon work from as wide a choice as possible. One of the compensations that comes from living at the present time is the wealth of art from vastly different civilizations and countries which is readily available to us. I would advise the serious student to approach it with as few preconceptions as possible. The unexpectedness of the artist's vision is on the one hand the thing for which society has the greatest admiration, but on the other for which they tend to have the least tolerance, if it runs counter to their established expectations. The man who is quoted as saying, 'I don't know much about it, but I know what I like', has become, quite rightly, a figure of fun, but I am afraid that too many genuine lovers of art tend to adopt a similar position by restricting themselves to the enjoyment of a limited range with which they are already familiar. I would advise you that, however doubtful you might be at first, you will ultimately benefit from as wide an appreciation of as great a variety of art forms as you can possibly achieve. When faced by the work of an unfamiliar artist or by a style to which at first sight you are unsympathetic, the important thing to remember is that the artist is not obliged to justify what he has done to anyone other than himself, and thus the onus is on you to try to understand what he is saying on his terms. This can involve you in a considerable amount of study and research but if you are tempted to dismiss his work too easily, remember that this would be a futile gesture; more often than not the artist will not know, and even if he did, why, in these circumstances should he care? I will admit that the thought that months, perhaps years, of his work can be dismissed so lightly is depressing to any artist but he can always be consoled by the knowledge of his own integrity, so if you do behave in this way it is your loss not his. I would like to emphasize that if you are going to develop as an artist, this is a loss you cannot afford. It is much better, if you find yourself in this situation, to reserve your judgement until you are sure that you have spent sufficient time for your decisions to be both informed and rational.

I am convinced that it is worthwhile spending time trying to evaluate work which is really not worth it, rather than running the risk of ignoring something which could eventually be of great benefit to you. Fortunately most of the basic concepts in art remain constant and it is only the style and preoccupations of different cultures that change. A genuine appreciation of the work from one period is a great help towards the understanding and enjoyment of work from any other. For this reason, I would advise the inexperienced sculptor to start by increasing his understanding of the work towards which he has a natural response.

2

# The studio

## The working environment

When one considers the wide range of activities which come under the general heading of sculpture, and the complexity of the various processes involved, it is reassuring to know that there are only a few items of basic equipment which the sculptor must have before he can start to practise his art. There are probably as many different ideal studios as there are sculptors and so in this chapter I propose to give only an outline of what is normally considered essential, plus a few items which can be usefully acquired as the need arises.

Most of the processes of sculpture are rather messy, and the artist functions best when he feels both free and comfortable, so in general it is better to work in a room set aside solely for use as a studio. If this is not possible, try to acquire a corner of a room which is not used for any other purpose and which does not serve as a passageway to other parts of one's living area. Most sculptors prefer to work in a large space, but the essential requirement is that the space chosen should allow ample room to stand back from the work in progress so that it can be seen as a whole. A level, solid floor which can be washed easily is a further advantage, especially if most of the work is to be modelled in clay. Easy access to a water supply is also important. (The ideal studio should be fitted with a special large casting sink equipped with a heavy duty sludge trap.) It is important to try for a light source which is as constant as possible – the traditional artist's north light provided by a top or skylight fully justifies its popularity. The judicious placing of artificial lights, particularly fluorescent tubes supplemented by a flexible spot, can help to extend the time available for working. I must admit, however, that I prefer to make all important decisions by daylight. If as much of the working area as possible is painted white this will help to make the most of the available light and prevent confusion when using colour on the sculptures. Mirrors can also be helpful in using the light to its best advantage as well as providing different views of the work and enabling the sculptor to use himself as a model when necessary.

## Equipment, materials and tools

Once a suitable working area has been chosen, the first important item of equipment is a good firm working bench. There are a number of proprietary brands available but an old-fashioned kitchen table, reinforced with angle brackets, makes a reasonable substitute. A series of boxes can be used on top of the table to achieve a comfortable working height for most small sculptures and a tabletop turntable will further increase one's ease of working. At a later stage the work bench can be supplemented with purpose-built modelling stands and bankers.

The studio should also be equipped with a generous amount of shelving to store completed and partially completed work as well as all the necessary tools and materials. One modern invention which has benefited sculptors enormously is polythene sheeting. The thin gauge is ideal for protecting and keeping damp work in progress, while the thicker sheets are very useful in protecting materials and equipment not actually in use,

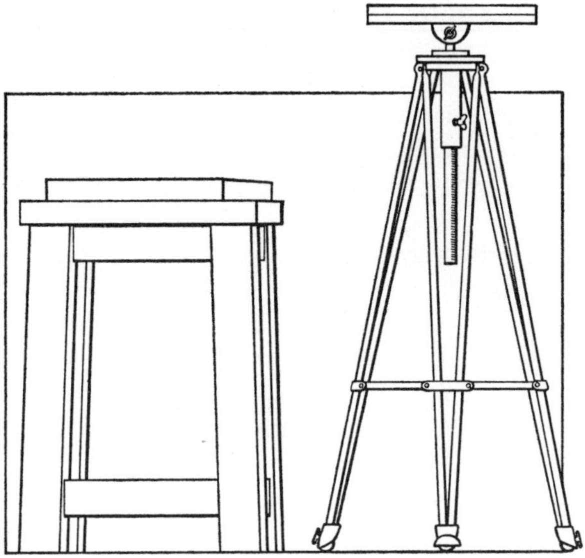

Figure 1 Banker and modelling stand

especially during the casting process. In most climates some form of heating will be necessary to add to the comfort of the artist but also, and more importantly, to prevent work in progress from freezing, which would cause irreparable damage. Some sculpture processes demand temperatures above a stated minimum and details will be given in later chapters where this is necessary.

Clay is an essential item in most studios and although it is usually bought prepared and ready for use it will need careful storage and occasional reconditioning if it is to be used properly. A system which allows this to be done should be adopted from the start. It will entail three separate rigid waterproof containers for each type of clay used. Galvanized buckets or dustbins complete with lids are very suitable for this purpose. Clay in current use is stored in one of these containers. Clay which has become too dry for comfortable working is stored in the second container, while the third is used for clay which has been allowed to thoroughly dry out and then soaked in water to recondition it. The usual procedure is to rotate the bins as the working clay is used up so that the reconditioned clay becomes in turn the working clay. The empty container becomes the dry clay bin and the previous dry clay bin becomes the reconditioning bin.

This system is ideal if a plaster drying slab is used to dry quickly the reconditioned clay to the required working consistency. A suitable drying slab can be easily made by filling a shallow box with plaster of paris mixed in the way described in chapter 9. Care should be taken at all times to keep the clay as clean as possible. Small amounts of dirty clay are better thrown away but larger quantities containing impurities can be sifted during the reconditioning process. The use of clay at varying consistencies to exploit fully its versatility only comes with practice, but the studio should be equipped to assist in the developing of this skill.

Plaster and *ciment fondu* should only be bought in small quantities as required. They must be stored in air-tight containers and kept well away from the water supply as they are easily spoiled if allowed to become damp. Special instructions for the safe storage of the materials used in polyester resin casting are given in chapter 11.

Other essential materials for which storage provision should be made are: shellac, wax polish, colouring agents, french chalk, plasterers' scrim, brass fencing and soft soap. Quite a lot of the materials used in the making of a sculpture, especially those used for the armature, can be salvaged and re-used. These include various pieces of seasoned timber, lead piping, aluminium, and galvanized and copper wire. These need not be stored in the immediate working area, but if some storage space is kept available it can save the sculptor considerable amounts of money. Special items such as casting wax and vinamould should be stored in a dry, dust-proof place. Most sculptors develop a magpie-like nature and love to save odd items on the basis that they might one day be useful. In my experience this often proves true and particularly applies to such things as nails, screws, washers, nuts and bolts, etc.

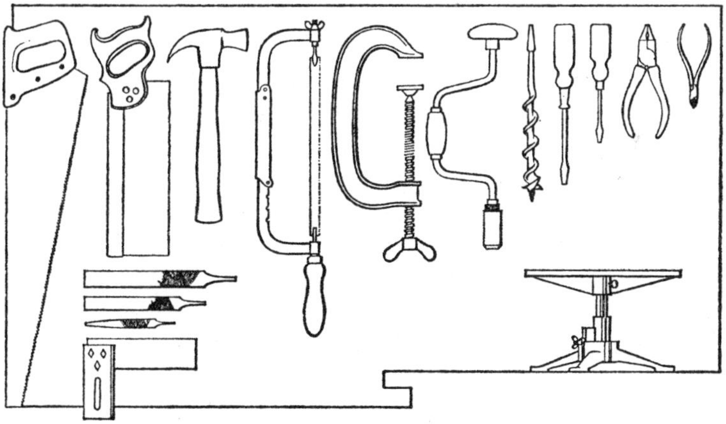

Figure 2 General purpose tools and a tabletop stand

Many of the tools used in sculpture are of a general purpose nature and can be quite easily obtained from a hardware supplier. This basic tool kit should include such things as a hammer, saw, screwdriver, hacksaw, pliers, wire cutters, knife, paint brushes, hand drill and bits. In addition to these general requirements some specialized tools and materials will also be necessary for the various sculpture processes. A set of boxwood modelling tools will greatly assist in the accurate applying of the clay during the modelling stage. A pair of callipers, a tape measure and a plumb line are essential for portrait work but they are also useful during the creative stages in any sculpture, especially when working from a maquette. During the casting process at least two polythene bowls and some pieces of sponge will be necessary. Other items essential at this stage include a firm bladed knife for cleaning the seams, a pair of sharp pointed scissors for accurately cutting up the brass fencing, and a pair of general purpose kitchen scissors for cutting the scrim and string when reinforcing the mould and tying the various pieces together. A light mallet weighing about eight ounces and a series of blunt chisels are also used in casting to chip the mould away from the completed cast.

During the finishing process most sculptures will need to be worked on with a series of sharp files and fine abrasives such as carborundum and sandpapers. I would also reserve a special set of paint brushes for use at this stage. The studio should be equipped at all times with a plentiful supply of polishing and cleaning cloths and, if possible, paper towels. Details of the specialized tools for welding, wood and stone carving are given in the appropriate chapters.

In the practice of sculpture the artist must use techniques and methods belonging to a whole range of different crafts. This means that there are a number of tools and pieces of equipment which, while not essential for the sculptor, can make his life much easier. An electric drill complete with the widest possible range of attachments is one of these time and labour saving additions to any studio. Further items which should be acquired if possible include a metal working vice, a set of G clamps, a spirit level, a blow lamp, a hand spray used to keep work in progress damp, and a hose attachment for use in cleaning out difficult moulds. A good camera, used properly, will prove invaluable to the sculptor. Accurate records of one's work showing it to the best advantage are usually necessary, in the early stages, when dealing with prospective clients. It is also very useful to be able to take the necessary photographs for reference when dealing with a subject which is not available for continued study.

When all the necessary tools, materials and pieces of equipment have been gathered together I feel that, unless one is of an incorrigibly puritan nature, it is also important to make the studio a comfortable place to be in. I find that a favourite chair and extension speakers from my record player provide an atmosphere in which I can both work and relax. This in turn often leads to a creative spell, at times when I would not have thought it possible.

3

# Making an armature

The essential difference between modelled sculptures and sculptures carved in either wood or stone is that in modelling the final form is built up piece by piece. Clay has always been a popular material for this process; it allows the sculptor to modify his design as required as well as providing the means for a wide range of textures and finishes. Although this malleable quality is very useful during the creative stages, it also means that the clay is too soft to be used for most sculptures, unless it is supported by a reinforced framework. This supporting structure around which the model is built is known as the armature.

In figure sculpture the armature can be thought of as a rather primitive skeleton. It has a similar structure and serves very much the same purpose. The armature is built on to a modelling board which must be considered as an important part of the whole support. It provides the foundation for the whole of the reinforcing framework and during the modelling process it will be subject to considerable stress. The strength of this construction can be only as strong as its weakest part. This board should always be made from well seasoned timber and if possible a hard wood should be used. Plywood and similar laminates are not suitable because the board will have to be kept damp for most of the time it is in use.

For large sculptures the board can be made from lengths of planking. A gap of about one-eighth of an inch left between each piece will minimize any effects caused by warping. All modelling boards should be raised up on two battens which add strength and enable the sculpture to be moved about more easily. The size of the board will vary depending on the size of the proposed sculpture, but it must be sufficiently large to ensure stability. There is nothing more nerve-racking than having to work on a sculpture which has become top heavy.

### Designing an armature

The first consideration in the design of a particular armature is that it must be strong enough to support the weight of the sculpture and rigid enough to allow the clay to be modelled without any unpleasant vibration. The various parts of the armature, however, should be designed so that they are flexible enough to allow the artist to benefit from the versatility of the clay. Although the artist should have a fairly clear idea of his intentions before he starts work it is not always easy or even desirable to be absolutely sure of the exact position and size of each form. The armature should, when possible, be designed so that the sculpture is built on to a clay bed. This will allow any desired changes in the height to be accommodated easily at a later stage.

A simple armature for a relief sculpture can be made if nails are driven into the modelling board and allowed to project above the clay bed in those areas where there is likely to be the greatest weight of clay. Unwanted nails can then be hammered below the clay surface at a later stage in the modelling and extra ones added as desired. For large relief sculptures or where a considerable bulk of clay must be supported extra reinforcing can be achieved by bridging the gap between the nail heads with strips of plasterer's lath or loops of wire. With free-standing sculptures the precise design of each armature will be determined by the requirements of each individual sculpture, but there are a series of traditional designs which if slightly adapted will be suitable for almost any sculptural situation.

To fulfil the requirements of strength plus flexibility already discussed these traditional designs make use of a combination of materials, including wood, mild steel, lead piping and square section aluminium. The usual system is for the lead and aluminium to support the clay and for the wood and mild steel to be fixed to the modelling board to support the whole. In figure modelling and similar sculptures, where a rigid support running up through the legs would inhibit the artist's freedom, a supporting iron which projects from the back or side of the model is used. It is placed in such a way that it interferes least with the articulation of the sculpture. Suitable back irons can be bought from a sculptor's supplier in a variety of sizes or they can be made from square section mild steel rod if the studio is equipped with a suitable metal-working vice. When used with large sculptures a wooden framework is attached to the back iron so that the weight of the clay is evenly distributed. In this case the support is improved if the wood is arranged so that clay can be forced between the pieces to form a solid core. The flexible part of armatures is traditionally made from lead piping but square section aluminium is also suitable for small models. The initial cost of these materials is quite high but this can be spread over a number of sculptures if the armatures are designed correctly and stored carefully.

## Assembling the armature

When assembling the armatures separate pieces of the chosen

material are used to support the various parts of the figure.

The traditional method is to use one length bent into shape and attached to the back iron to support the legs and torso. Extra pieces are then added to reinforce the arms and a further piece which runs down through the figure and along the back iron provides the main support for the head and neck. Extra strengthening to this basic armature can then be added as

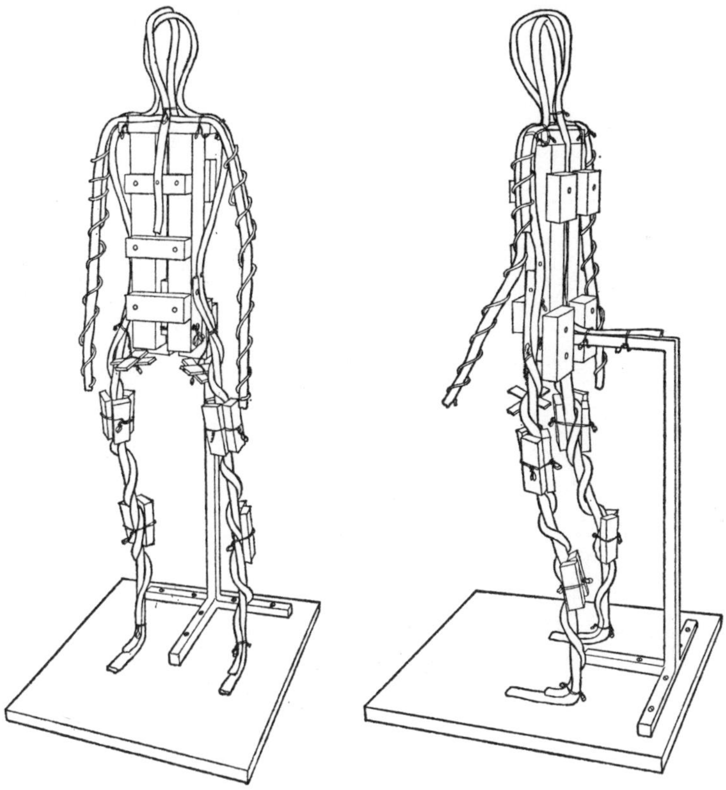

Figures 3 and 4 Lead and wood armature supported on a back iron suitable for a life size figure

required. Crossed strips of plasterer's lath suspended on twisted wire, known in sculpture as butterflies, are hung from the existing framework to support areas of extra clay weight. The design of some sculptures will allow the supporting irons to run up through the figure without unduly restricting the artist's freedom to make later modifications. In this case, to prevent difficulties in the casting, it is advisable to use separate pieces of iron for each leg. These should overlap each other at the shoulders, where they can be tied together.

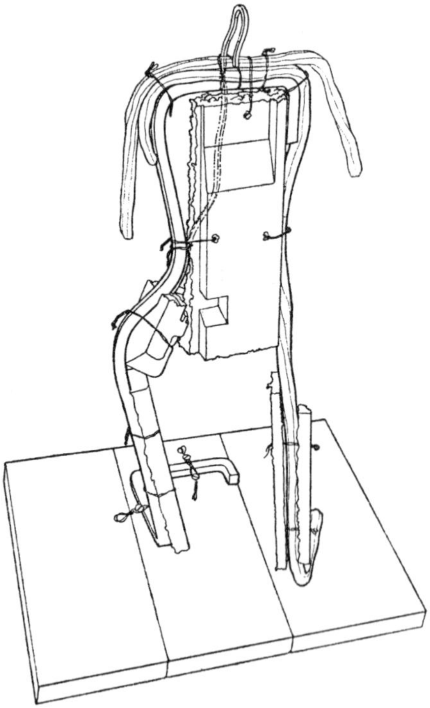

Figure 5 Lead and polystyrene torso armature on a fixed iron support

Similar skeleton structures can be made from thin aluminium to form the armature for very small sculptures or maquettes. The traditional armature for a portrait head or bust uses two separate loops of lead or aluminium, bent to the shape of the neck and skull, and fixed to the modelling board by a length of wood. These wooden supports, known as head pegs, can be bought specially designed for the sculptor with a bolt running through their length and a socket attachment for fixing to the board. If desired a similar support can be easily made from a length of two-by-two timber fastened to the board with four strong right-angle brackets.

To prevent the armature from interfering with the modelling the lead or aluminium should be attached to the wood so

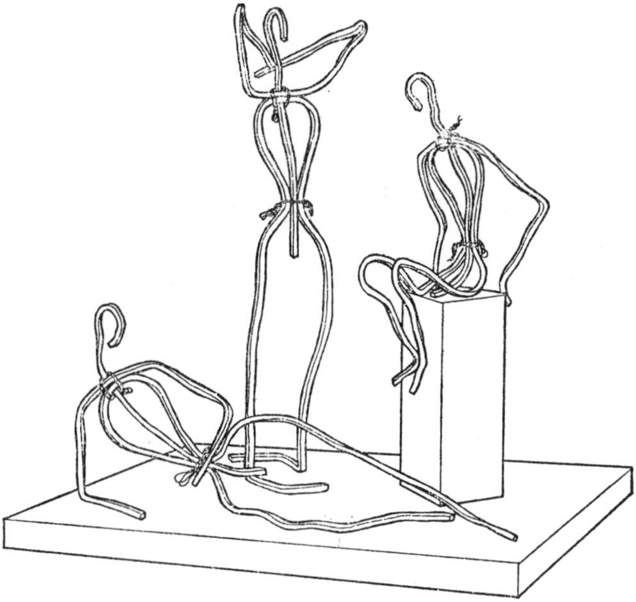

Figure 6 Aluminium armatures for maquettes and small sculptures

that the top of the head peg lies just below the pit of the neck. The head peg should always be long enough to allow at least part of the shoulders to be modelled so that the exact termination of the form can be decided upon at a late stage in the modelling when the most suitable design can be more clearly seen. If a major part of the shoulders is to be included as part of the final sculpture, strips of wood should be attached to the head peg to support the extra weight of clay. An armature

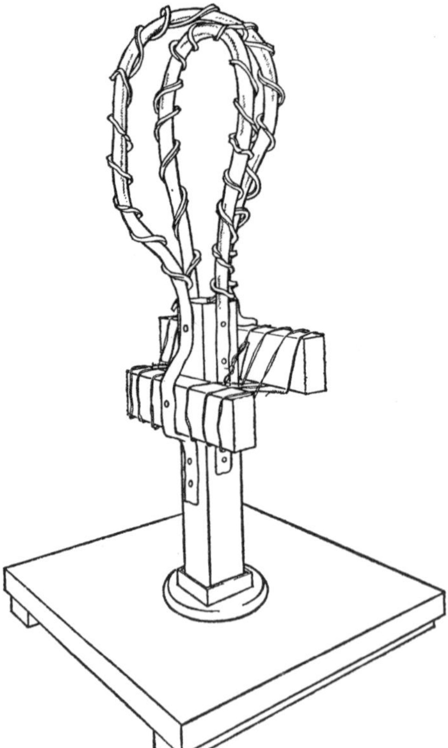

Figure 7 Armature for a portrait head

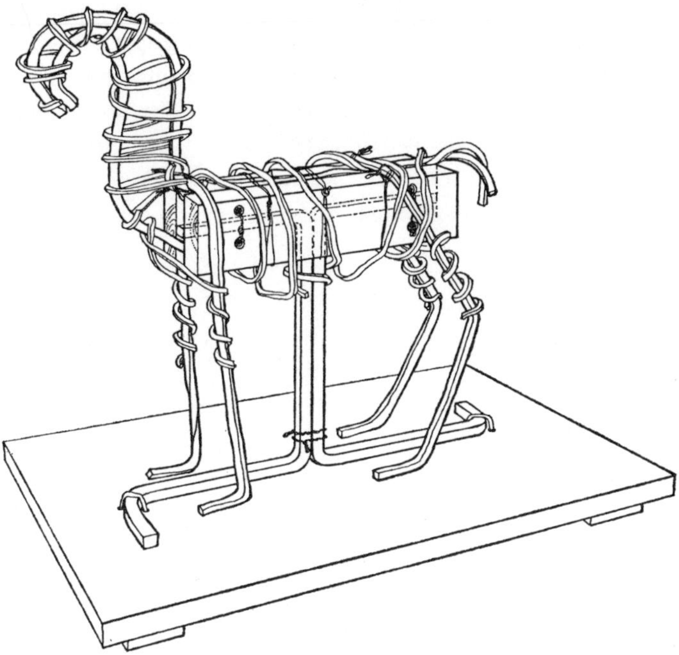

Figure 8 Armature for a horse

suitable for an animal sculpture, where the weight is apparently taken on four thin legs, can be designed using a similar method so that previously described for use with a back iron. In this case the supporting iron, which should project from the underside of the model, will probably have to be bent into shape by the sculptor.

## Taking the armature apart

One important design feature which affects all armatures is that it will have to be taken apart at a later stage during the casting process when the clay is removed from the mould.

Quite often this has to be done in difficult circumstances, but with care these difficulties can be kept to a minimum. Whenever it is possible, without seriously weakening the structure the armature is made up from separate pieces which can be later removed individually from the mould. The various pieces should always be tied together rather than welded so that they can be separated easily. Taking the armature apart is also made

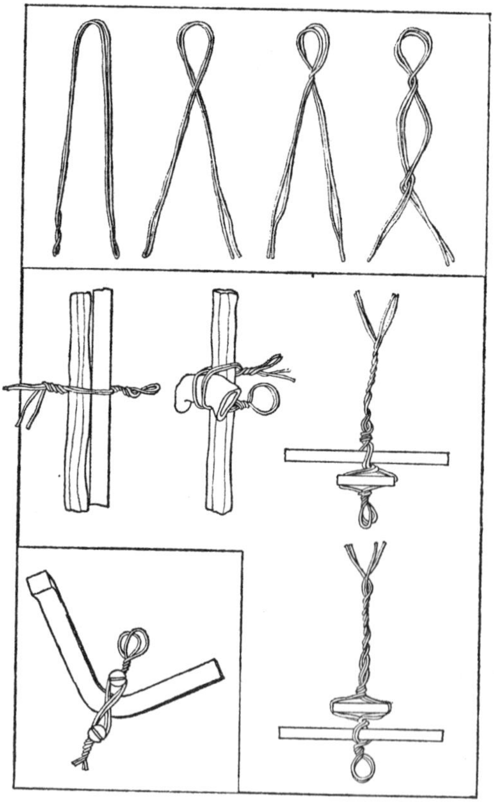

Figure 9 Special wire knot used for all armature fastenings

much easier if the same sculptor's knot is used for all fastenings. Thus by being constant a knot can be untied easily even if it cannot be clearly seen. For the same reason thin copper wire which remains flexible should be used for all fastenings but if this is not available galvanized wire can be used as a substitute. If possible all knots should be tied at the back of the armature because in the traditional method of casting this will be the area with the greatest degree of access.

## Armatures for plaster and cement models

Armatures designed on similar principles can be used as reinforcements for work modelled direct in more permanent materials such as plaster and cement. As, however, these materials do not have the flexibility of clay, and as the strength of the supporting structure will be expected to last indefinitely, a more rigid armature is preferred. In this case mild steel rods, carefully bent into shape are substituted for the lead or aluminium supports previously described. Again because the work is being undertaken in a permanent material the use of a back iron or other projecting support should be avoided. With this type of work a chicken wire cage is sometimes built on top of the more traditional armature to give extra reinforcing and to reduce the weight of the finished sculpture. Whenever the armature is to form an actual part of the finished work it must be effectively sealed against rust before being used.

4

# Figure modelling and composition

This chapter is designed mainly for the person with an interest in figurative work and especially for the person who is unable to work directly from a life model. When it is possible to work from a model the general method outlined in chapter 5 can be followed. I suggest that for the beginner a sculpture of a torso would make a suitable starting point. At first sight this might seem an odd choice of subject but there are many historical precedents and the way in which it enables us to deal easily with so many of the important aspects of sculpture makes it ideal.

A torso consists of the main part of the body without the head but with sufficient indications of the arms and legs to give interest to the composition. It is made up of very simple large forms which are easy to recognize and contains enough delicate details to satisfy anyone whose interest lies in this direction. It is easy to use one's own body for reference both by touch and by looking in a mirror and even more important by actually moving and so feeling the areas of articulation. The torso by its nature will tend to produce a compact simple sculpture which will serve as an easy introduction to the purely technical aspects of modelling such as putting up the armature and casting the sculpture into a permanent material. The main interest in all sculptures, regardless of style, should be integral

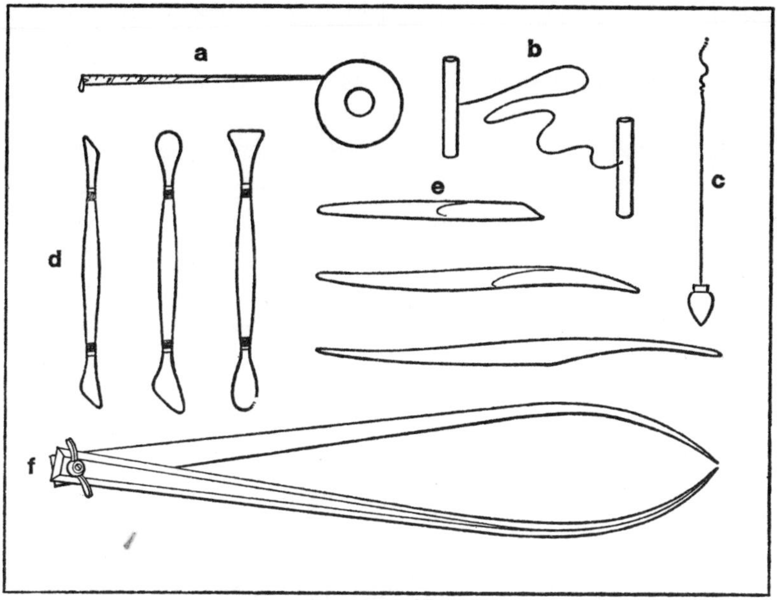


Figure 10 Basic tools used in modelling:
a, tape measure; b, cheese wire; c, plumb line; d, wire ended tools; e, boxwood tools; f, callipers

rather than illustrative or theatrical, and the restrictions imposed by a torso tend to make this point obvious.

A little practice will serve to demonstrate the pointlessness of making a torso which attempts to tell a story, such as a torso of someone running for a bus or, even more impossible, a torso playing Hamlet. This does not mean that references to outside events are necessarily bad but that they must at all times be subservient to the actual nature of the sculpture. The relationship of the various parts of the composition, the tension that exists between forms, the interplay of different weights, and the rhythms they establish in the overall design, are the basic qualities of a sculpture to which we respond.

In order to fully explore the three-dimensional possibilities it is usual to make a series of small sketch models before starting on the full-scale work. As we have already learned, these small sketch models are known as maquettes. If used properly maquettes will genuinely explore the limits of a particular subject and will help the artist to avoid the limiting effects of his possible preconceptions. The aspect of discovery is just as important as the final communication of the findings. Indeed, an enthusiastic research into almost any subject will generate sufficient impetus for the creative process to operate. To do this job properly the maquettes should be small and both easy and quick to make. The tendency to make small finished sculptures at this stage must be avoided or the translation of the idea into a larger scale will be both unnecessary and a laborious mechanical process. When making sketch models for a torso it should be possible to produce at least ten variations in an hour. If this proves difficult it will be due to an excess of self-consciousness rather than lack of talent. Avoid unnecessary detail and remember that there is no need to worry about making mistakes at this stage.

In a torso the two main forms are the upper part, which is mainly the rib cage, and the lower part formed by the pelvis. By moving one's own body it becomes obvious that these two parts can be moved independently of each other. As we begin to explore the possibilities this suggests it is important to make a separate maquette for each variation as it occurs. Two simple blocks roughly in the correct proportion will be sufficient to indicate each position the rib cage and pelvis can achieve in their relationship. If we next consider that the legs can move independently of both each other and the pelvis a further series of variations will be suggested. Two small pieces of clay will serve to indicate these on the maquettes. Similar pieces of clay can then be used to serve as the arms. As we can again articulate the arms independently of each other and also contrast these movements with the existing variations of the rib cage, pelvis and legs it becomes possible to produce a vast range of maquettes in a very short time. Most of these maquettes, because of the experimental nature of the method, will be either uninteresting or unsuitable for development and at the conclusion of this stage can be returned to the clay bin.

Selecting the final maquette from those not discarded is a much more difficult task. The main points to consider are: do the variations in a particular combination enhance each other, and does the composition achieve an overall balance? Parts of the composition can complement each other by repeating similar movements in different forms or by contrasting one movement with another. Simple compositions with very little movement can, of course, be just as successful as others with more dramatic contrasts. A purely visual balance is all that is necessary in sculpture but for the beginner it might be safer if an actual physical balance is achieved.

Once the final maquette has been selected it must be allowed to dry out slowly and then sealed with a series of coats of diluted shellac. This will help to preserve it but it will remain fragile and must be treated with care. A good protection is to keep it in a small box lined with cotton wool when it is not in use. Some artists, for ease of working and storage, prefer to make their maquettes in either plasticine or modelling wax and the beginner will probably wish to experiment until a personal preference is found.

If the proposed sculpture is not going to be very large, say up to twenty-four inches, then this type of maquette will be the only preparatory work necessary. For larger sculptures it is usual to extend the preparation by making a larger sketch model, known as the working model. This should be to a definite proportion of the proposed sculpture. The final maquette or the working model is first used in the design of a suitable armature, details of which are given in chapter 3.

## Modelling technique

The modelling technique is essentially a building process and, using the maquette as a guide, the sculpture proper is started by building up the clay on to the armature. The first clay applied must be pressed firmly into and around the framework to ensure stability. Although clay is an extremely versatile medium, it does not lend itself easily to carving, so it is very important to avoid getting too great a bulk of clay too soon. The sculptor must control his medium and the unthinking application of clay can be most unproductive and difficult to correct.

If by some mischance the sculpture is over-built in the early stages, it is better to cut one's losses, take it all off the armature

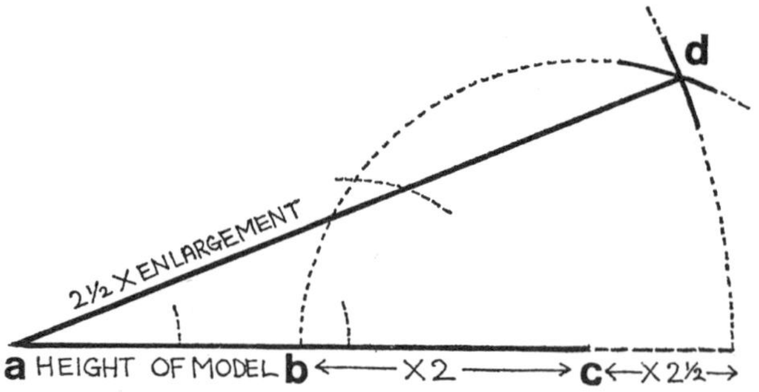


Figure 11 Diagram of a scale for enlarging $2\frac{1}{2}$ times
Draw a line a-b-c equal to twice the height of the model to be enlarged. Place the points of the calipers at b and c and describe an arc from c above the line a-b-c. Reset the calipers to a measurement $2\frac{1}{2}$ times the height of the model and describe an arc from a to cross the first arc at d. Draw a line a-d.
To use this scale take any caliper measurement from the model and mark it off twice on the line a-b-c. Describe an arc from the second point to cross the line a-d. Distances from a to the points where the arcs intersect the line a-d give the enlarged measurements.

and start again. This might appear to be a brutal decision but it is better in the end because the hopeful pushing about of unwanted clay will eventually lead to complete frustration. This type of decision is made much easier if the loving modelling of detail is avoided until it is absolutely certain that all the major forms are correct. A controlled method of modelling can be easily achieved if the sculptor constantly asks himself where and why each piece of clay should be added.

The translation of the maquette into a larger scale is a difficult undertaking and the inexperienced sculptor must not become too depressed when these difficulties are encountered. Practice is all-important and the suggested exercises for train-

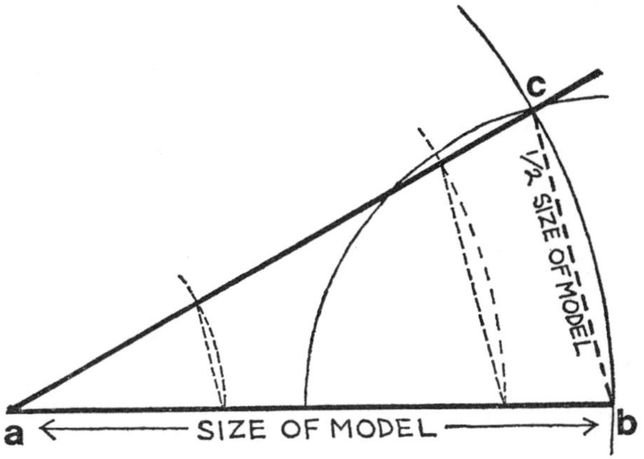


Figure 12 Diagram of a scale for reducing by one half
Draw a line a-b equal to the height of the original model. With the points of the calipers on a and b describe an arc from a above the line a-b. Reset the calipers to a measurement equal to one half the height of the model and describe an arc from b to intersect the first arc at c. Draw a line a-c.
To use this scale take any caliper measurement from the model and describe an arc from a to cross both lines a-b and a-c. A straight line distance between the intersecting points will be proportionate measurement for one half size of the model

ing the eye given in chapter 1 should prove helpful at this stage. The increase in scale will also be easier if the sculpture is made a specific number of times larger than the maquette so that definite measurements can be taken from any part and translated accurately. A pair of callipers, which are designed to take measurements from three-dimensional forms, will be very useful at this stage. These can be supplemented by a plumb line which, by providing a visual straight edge, enables us to locate points accurately in relation to each other.

When one is working from a maquette there is often a temptation to modify the original design. This is a very difficult point on which to advise because some modification will be necessary due to the change in scale. For the inexperienced sculptor I would suggest that it is better to be guided by the maquette at least until all the major areas of the form are established. If at an earlier stage one is convinced that the ideas in the maquette are no longer valid, the best thing would be to leave the sculpture for a little while to make a further

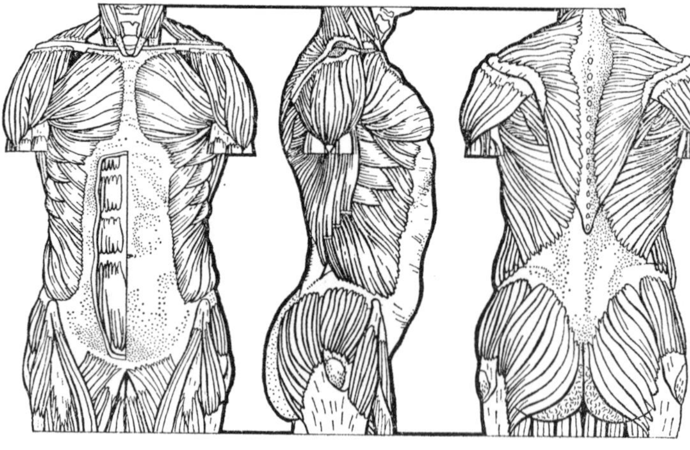

Figure 13 The anatomy of a torso

series of maquettes exploring the new ideas. In the long term this can save a great deal of time and wasted effort. Irretrievable decisions about the future of any sculpture must not be made at the end of the day when one is bound to be tired. There will also be occasions when a coffee break is the best immediate solution to a particular problem.

It is usually necessary to include slightly more detail in the final sculpture compared with the maquette. If the artist is very much concerned with a representative approach, a knowledge of anatomy will prove very useful at this stage. For most people this will have to be acquired from books and it is very important that these are used properly. A purely academic knowledge is more likely to be inhibiting than useful. This can be avoided if the book is consulted only in relation to specific points as they occur; much more importance should be placed on the shapes and connections of the bones and muscles than on their Latin names.

## Texture

As one approaches the final stages in the work a concern for texture becomes important. If the clay has been modelled correctly and the sculpture built up piece by piece, the work will already have a genuine texture resulting from the process. Most final textures make use of this and are a development of the modelling technique. The use of texture and the consequent breaking up of the light reflected from the surface gives us the opportunity to distinguish between the apparent hardness and softness of different areas. The usual procedure is to model the form tighter, that is to a smoother finish, where the bone lies nearest to the surface. Variations of texture can also be used to indicate different areas of colour but this must be done with discretion so that it does not become crude or interfere with the unity of the form.

As well as the texture which comes from the modelling process it is possible to use a whole range of artificial textures by lightly pressing such things as coke, rough sponge, pumice stone and tree bark etc. against the surface of the clay. This type of texture must be used with restraint and a prior study of different natural textures is advisable. Unless the final sculpture is designed to be highly polished, an absolutely smooth finish is never desirable and under no circumstances should water be used directly to achieve a smooth surface as the resultant used soap effect is very unpleasant.

Clay of a reasonably firm consistency will be necessary for most of the stages in the modelling but experiments with softer clay can often help in achieving an exciting tactile finish. A knowledge of the material in which the work is to be cast, and a study of other sculptures in these materials, is also helpful in deciding at just what stage the modelling is complete. The modelling of a torso, or indeed of any sculpture, is a relatively lengthy process and it is very important to keep the clay in perfect condition right up to the moment when the first coat of plaster is applied in the casting. Work in progress must always be stored in a completely sealed polythene bag which must be checked regularly for small tears and holes. During the actual modelling the work should be lightly sprayed with water at frequent intervals. To avoid damage this will mean interrupting the work until the surface has slightly dried but unless too much water has been used this will only be a few minutes. Large quantities of water must never be poured over the modelling, even in cases where it has been accidentally allowed to become too dry. If the work has to be stored for long periods or kept in a place where it might be vulnerable it can be protected by a polythene covered wood reinforced cage.

### The making of images

One of man's unique characteristics is his ability to respond, not only to reality, but also to images of himself and his experiences. The popularity of television demonstrates that this response can be keenly aroused even though the images differ considerably in terms of size and colour from our normal experience. The artist has traditionally made use of this acceptance and consequently most historical sculpture is concerned with the making of images. Although the advances recently made in technology have provided us with a number of new vehicles for the expression of these images, and this has to some extent modified the approach of the sculptor to his art, it has in no way invalidated what is loosely known as figurative work. It simply means that the artist has a greater range of conventions at his disposal and that he must decide which is the best means of communicating a particular concept.

The person interested in developing a figurative approach to sculpture can extend the style and method of working used with the torso to include more complex situations. The use of the whole figure and then groups of figures will provide a much greater opportunity to use the articulation of the various parts to balance, contrast and comment on each other. This extension of the inherent possibilities does, of course, call for an equal development of control and sensitivity. The careful study of gesture and facial expression and a knowledge of the compositional devices traditionally used by other sculptors will be of great assistance. For example, the way in which Greek sculpture displays a superb ability to combine the suggestions of movement with the essentially static nature of the medium can be applied to the most modern subject matter.

A further aspect of composition which the artist must consider is the relationship between his figures and their environment. In some sculptures this takes the form of an equal concern for the space which the figures occupy, in others the figures are placed in a real situation or in a full-scale constructed environment. This area is particularly exciting when the artist avoids the danger of producing sentimental or superficial work by dealing with a situation which is part of his everyday life. In order to maintain a constant flow of ideas it is advisable to keep a notebook and sketchbook to record all items of interest as well as studies related to work currently in progress. These can be usefully supplemented by a scrapbook collection of interesting photographs.

The actual modelling of a figure composition can present considerable technical difficulties. It will be necessary to first design a suitable armature and the artist must also remain aware that he will eventually have to cast the completed work. If a sculpture of a torso has been successfully completed the sculptor should have a reasonable knowledge of his present capabilities. The design of the first figure composition must take into account this knowledge. In most cases this must act as a restraint and for the person to whom this would be too frustrating I would suggest working on a relief sculpture. This would, by making the least possible technical demands, allow the artist to extend his ambition to the greatest possible degree.

## Style and content – mother and child compositions

The ultimate character of any work of art is determined by the personality of the artist, the chosen medium, and the accepted traditions of a particular period. Within certain broad categories, however, the intention of the artist can be related directly to and assisted by his choice of style. The person taking up sculpture is advised to study the relationship between style and content which exists in all sculpture.

This relationship can be very clearly seen in the variety of compositions based on the popular theme of mother and child. In their treatment of this subject artists have, by their selection and treatment of the pose and character of individual forms, and through their choice of gesture and expression, realized very different intentions, while retaining the essential nature of the relationship. Many artists, by using a standard formalized hieratic composition, have transformed this subject into a portrayal of the Madonna and Child. In these sculptures the formal nature of the composition is used to suggest that the relationship is of a different order to the purely natural. Other artists, by selecting a composition which emphasizes the general aspects of the mother and child relationship, produce sculptures of an idealized nature to comment on the universal aspects of maternity.

This subject has also been used by artists primarily concerned with abstract sculptural qualities. In this type of work the artist again subjugates the natural elements to exploit the inherent possibilities of composing a large form in relation to a small one, making use of the structural relationships that exist between both forms. The most natural portrayals of this subject seek to establish the personal relationship between a particular mother and her child. This method of approach relates strongly to the area of portraiture where the artist is excited by the possibilities in individual forms and expressions. In this type of composition a concern for the sculptural nature of the work is shown by the careful selection from an observed range of possibilities rather than, as was the case in the previous examples, the imposing of a predetermined compositional order. Many sculptures, of course, manage to combine successfully elements of each different approach but this is always better achieved by an awareness of the possibilities in each.

5

# Portraiture

## The model

Of all the many branches in sculpture, portraiture is the one which imposes the most obvious and definite discipline on the artist. As a result of this, it is in some ways the easiest and in others the most difficult subject for the sculptor. The fact that his source of information remains constant and readily available and that the area of selection is kept within narrow limits helps the artist to concentrate the whole of his energy in one direction. The difficulty is that this energy must concern itself with a strictly accurate observation and rendering of a subtle and complex form. Success results from a genuine concern for and response to the individuality of personal forms and expressions.

Portraiture can of course deal with the whole figure and, in rare cases, with whole groups of figures, and although today it more usually takes the form of a portrait head or bust, the method of working described in this chapter can be applied to the whole field of figure modelling when the study is informed by the observation of a particular model. It is the nature of this working relationship between the artist and the model which gives to portraiture its unique characteristic. Consequently the first important consideration in the practice of this art is the choice of model. In many cases, because of the associated element of patronage, the artist will have very little choice unless he is both famous and financially independent but if possible the inexperienced sculptor should choose a person with a prominent and obvious bone structure. Fortunately this is very often found in older people.

Once the model has been chosen, it is very important for the artist to establish a good working relationship. A concern for the personality and comfort of the sitter, coupled with a serious attitude during the working periods, is most likely to be successful. The choice of pose is particularly important and this should be arrived at by a careful study of the person's natural movements. It is most unfair and normally unproductive to force a model into an uncomfortable preconceived position. It is unlikely that the sitter, unless one is working with a professional model, will be able to say, with any accuracy, whether or not a particular pose is going to remain comfortable for any length of time. A few trial runs before starting the actual modelling can save a lot of future disagreement and frustration.

A professional sculptor's model will expect ten minutes' rest in each hour plus one fifteen minute tea or coffee break in a session lasting three hours. An inexperienced sitter might need longer or more frequent breaks and in this case the artist must control his natural impatience. It is much better to work for a shorter time when one is in full control and with the complete co-operation of the model.

The sculptor must have an exact knowledge of the chosen pose so that it can be reset accurately after each rest. If the nature of the pose and the reasons for its selection are carefully explained, the model will also be able to help in the resetting. It is usual to mark any point where the model comes into contact with the environment and the position of any relevant piece of furniture which might be accidentally moved. Whenever possible the subject should be at the same height as the work in progress. In portraiture, as the model is usually seated, a special throne or arrangement of sturdy boxes is often necessary to bring the sitter to a height at which the artist can comfortably work. Good lighting is also very important and it is particularly helpful if a similar light to that falling on the sitter also falls on the sculpture. A revolving throne and modelling stand will help to make the most of the available light, which should be as constant as possible.

Portraiture, like most other forms of sculpture, is a fairly lengthy process and it is important that the model understands this from the beginning. It is also helpful if the model can be persuaded to keep the same hair style and in the case of a portrait bust, wear the same clothes throughout the whole period of the work. The judicious use of selected items of jewellery, medals, etc. can add considerable interest to the sculpture and assist the artist to portray the character as well as the appearance of his subject.

The number of sittings necessary to complete the modelling of the sculpture will of course vary, depending on the experience and temperament of the artist, but as a rough guide I would suggest that a minimum of at least six three-hour sittings are likely to be necessary. If the sitter cannot be available for this length of time, a lot of the work can be done from photographs. This will also apply when attempting portraits of very young children, who cannot be expected to co-operate over such long periods. In both cases, a minimum of six special photographs, supplemented by at least two three-hour sittings will be necessary. The photographs should consist of one detailed full front, two of three-quarter views and two in profile, and one back view. These photographs should be taken under the direction of the sculptor and must include the whole neck and a little of the shoulders. They must be straightforward and accurate shots, taken on eye level and concerned solely with an accurate detailed record. One sitting will then be necessary for the sculptor to establish the exact shape and accurate measurement of all the basic forms. Using the photographs as a guide the artist can then translate these measurements into a simple formal structure of the head and neck. A second sitting will be necessary to obtain accurate information of the more detailed characteristics. Providing the photographs are clear it should then be possible to complete the portrait using the information they supply. If any extra sittings are possible these should be taken at an early stage in the work. It is of course possible to make exciting compositions based entirely on photographs and general information but it is unlikely that these will be accurate enough to call portraits.

### Beginning the sculpture

Clay is the usual medium employed for the actual modelling of a portrait. Wax or a similar malleable substance can also be used, but the direct modelling in a permanent material such as plaster or polyester resin is not generally recommended because these do not have the flexibility which is necessary in this exacting art. The armature for the clay sculpture is first bent into shape so that it follows exactly the inside form of the chosen pose. The correct relationship between the head and the neck must be established at this stage. It is useful to remember that whatever the position of the head the angle of the neck always slopes in a forward direction. It is impossible, without doing irreparable damage, to straighten the human neck and an attempt to do this seems to be the most common failing on the part of inexperienced sculptors.

Once the armature is in the correct position, the clay can be applied by pressing it firmly into and around the structure. As with most types of modelled sculpture, it is very important not to arrive over-quickly at too great a bulk of clay. Many people are misled by the apparent importance of the features into modelling them in detail before the basic structure is established. It is also worth remembering that only in rare cases are the features as large as they are important. When I was a student it was pointed out to me that I could recognize people quite easily at a distance that made it impossible to distinguish their features. This demonstrates clearly that each head has a definite structural character which must be first established in any successful portrait.

In the first sittings it is important to ignore the features altogether and to concentrate entirely on establishing this structure. The accurate modelling of this and indeed of all the forms in the figure is made much easier by the use of callipers which enable detailed measurements to be taken from all three-dimensional forms. These measurements can be translated most easily onto the sculpture if it is made to a life-size scale. An orderly method of working, that is of both applying the clay and of taking and using the measurements, is the one characteristic which above all others leads to success in this field. Accurate measurements become necessary as soon as the clay is built up on to the armature, to the stage where the basic form of the head and neck is recognizable. These early measurements should be taken from the areas where the bone structure is close to the surface because these points are more likely to remain constant.

To start taking measurements we must have one point which we accept as being accurate and fixed so that all the other points can be related to this constant. On a portrait head the chin is a popular choice for this first point. Using the fixed point as a reference a series of measurements are taken all round the head, two separate measurements being necessary to establish any one point accurately because it is necessary to fix the position of a particular form in relation to other forms as well as establishing its relative size.

I would like to stress once again the importance of first modelling correctly the largest areas of form. To do this it is necessary to establish the following points as soon as possible. The distance from the chin to the hair line, which determines the overall length of the face, and the distance between the chin and the eyebrows, which indicates the area in which all the features must be accommodated. It is then necessary to build up the brow in relation to the projection of the chin so that a further series of measurements can be taken to establish the length of the skull. By again taking measurements from the front or back and relating these to others taken from the profile it becomes possible to fix other such important points as the relative size and position of the cheekbone, jaw and neck. The sculptor then continues to use this comparative method of measuring forms to deal progressively with areas of greater detail and complexity.

It is very important, at this stage, for the artist to avoid the temptation of concentrating in any one area for too great a length of time; a methodical method of working, dealing with each form in turn, must be maintained. The experienced artist always tries to retain the liberty to make any necessary alterations with a minimum loss of detailed work. This lack of attention to relatively unimportant details in the early stages also allows points to be marked clearly by incised lines and small pieces of clay.

Although accurate measurement is extremely helpful to the sculptor, in the final analysis it is whether the sculpture looks right or not that is the vital point. At all stages the artist must continue to use his eye in evaluating the success or failure of his work. It is pointless to console oneself by saying that although a form looks wrong it must be correct because it was measured accurately. In most cases it will be found that, even if a measurement was originally correct, it has been changed in the subsequent modelling. To avoid this it is necessary to evaluate and re-check all the measurements regularly as the work progresses. The opposite situation, where the form looks correct even though inaccurately measured, is a much rarer phenomenon, and while it can occur, I would warn the beginner against the danger of taking artistic licence to the point of self-deception.

## Some practical hints

One aspect of sculpture which I find a constant source of interest is that although the size and character of individual features can vary enormously, they nevertheless maintain a relationship within each individual framework. An awareness of this can be used as a rough guide to the general proportions of any particular subject. This, when used in conjunction with the previously described system of measurement, will help the person taking up portraiture to avoid the most common pitfalls. I must emphasize that this is only a rough guide and all the relationships given must be taken as approximate.

In general it will be found that a line drawn across the centre of the eyes will divide the whole mass of the head in half. The distance from the hair line to the chin is the same as the overall length of the skull. The separation between the eyes is equal to the width of one eye. The top of the ears lines up with the brows while the tip of the lobe lines up with the nostrils. The corner of the mouth falls under the centre of the eye. The distance between the outside corners of the eyes is the same as the distance from the corner of the eye to the lower lip. The bottom of the lower lip is on a line half-way between the nose and the chin. The width of the mouth is equal to the length of the nose. I am sure that the perceptive student will be able to find other similar relationships which are particularly useful during the early stages. The establishing of this type of relationship can of course be useful in all the other fields of sculpture as well as in portraiture.

As the work is brought gradually to a conclusion the artist must again concern himself with the question of texture and the treatment of such forms as the eyes and hair, which because of their nature demand a certain amount of purely sculptural interpretation. It is in the treatment of these points that the greatest stylistic difference between individual artists and sculptures from different cultures are most clearly seen. The treatment of the eyes in particular can greatly determine the overall character of the sculpture and the sculptor will use this in relation to the character as well as the physical characteristics of his model. The depth of undercutting and the substitution of a hollow for the iris can be used to establish or to emphasize a suitable expression. The depth of the cutting can, if used sensitively, indicate the colour of the eyes as well as their expression.

One particular problem which often faces the portrait sculptor in this century is the treatment of spectacles in the case where the sitter wears them habitually. It is of course impossible to obtain a true likeness unless the artist is prepared to portray the normal appearance of his subject and, although one is often tempted, it is pointless to evade the problem by requesting the sitter to remove them. In general the inclusion of just sufficient indications of the frames will be enough to establish the character, but in special cases, where the lenses are very thick, the sculptor, with an exceedingly delicate touch, can indicate this by slightly blurring the modelling of the eye.

The colour and texture of the hair can be indicated by the textural treatment of the surface. In general a smooth slightly polished surface will create the impression of a fair or blond person. Skilled use of actual colour in the patination of the final cast can be used to further enhance these effects but this form of stylization must be used sensitively and under no circumstances should it interfere with or distort the form.

The whole art of portraiture rests to some extent on the general acceptance of certain conventions and the normal visitor to an exhibition of this type of work does not think of the sculptures as evidence of a concern with decapitation. The sensitive artist is, however, aware of this possibility and gives considerable attention to the termination of his forms. The relationship of the sculpture to its base or plinth can be very important in this respect. One method, which I have found to be very successful, is to model slightly more of the figure than is intended for the finished sculpture and to design the final cutting in relation to a mock-up of the proposed base.

6

# Stylized and abstract sculpture

## Stylization

All sculpture, regardless of its period or particular culture, contains elements of both stylization and abstraction. Even in sculpture of a highly representational nature, there are always some aspects of the subject which it is impossible to portray and others which can be portrayed only through the general acceptance of a convention or style. The fact that in a natural state all situations are dependent on each other involves the artist in a form of abstraction as soon as he makes any kind of selection. However complex a sculpture might be, it is bound to be simple compared with the complexities of nature and so the artist is forced further and further into the area of abstraction as his choice progresses and his knowledge is increased.

For most of the history of sculpture, the artist has been content to work mainly within the accepted traditions of his period and to extend its conventions only gradually. This has meant that their work has, in general, been eventually accepted by most people aware of and interested in the arts. This acceptance has been put under great strain by the majority of artists working in this century because they have taken the areas of stylization and abstraction as the major consideration of their sculpture. The decline of official patronage, with the consequent lessening of both restrictions and security, has led to a vast increase in the number of artists forced to look primarily towards other artists working in similar fields for acceptance and encouragement. This in turn has led to a greater concern for and questioning of the most fundamental aspects of their art. This situation has been further encouraged by the nature of our society which has been forced to reconsider its most cherished beliefs and assumptions by the rapid advances made in the fields of science, technology and communications.

The European tradition, extending from the Renaissance, of using the stylistic elements in sculpture to subordinate the actual material to the nature of the image, reached a climax towards the end of the last century with the work of Rodin. The success of his technique in deceiving the eye has sometimes resulted in an unawareness of just how much stylization this involved. The degree of stylization in the work of Brancusi, however, is much more apparent because it is applied to a completely different end. In most of his work the form of the subject is radically simplified in order to bring into prominence the actual nature of the sculptural material.

This concern for the sculpture as an object, rather than as a vehicle for an image, has been the prime interest of most sculptors during the first half of this century. In general, the materials of sculpture are radically different from the material and nature of the image portrayed. This means that artists working with a concept of truth to material are forced to adopt a major stylization of their subject.

The most obvious manifestation of this stylization is the selective simplification of the original image. This is in fact an extension of an accepted sculptural tradition and is only revolutionary in the extent to which it is taken. The person taking up sculpture who is interested in this field must remember, however, that in order to be successful any simplification must be based on knowledge. It must deal with the essential elements of the subject when, with a genuine understanding, it will be possible to make a clear rather than a superficial statement. There is also the risk of making an unintentional humorous sculpture unless the same degree of stylization is maintained throughout the whole composition. It is of course the unintentional rather than the humorous aspect to which one should object.

A further use of stylization is made in sculpture of an expressionistic nature where the original image is distorted to convey a greater degree of emotion than would be otherwise possible. By using a process of selection and stylization it is also possible to combine, in one sculpture, the knowledge and emotional reactions that the artist has felt towards a number of different natural situations. This is one of the features of the work of Henry Moore, particularly in those sculptures which relate both to the reclining female figure and to moorland landscape. It is very important to understand that this is an entirely different situation to a figure in a landscape. In this case the sculpture is both a figure and a landscape at the same time. Because of the increased awareness which has resulted from this contemporary interest in stylization, many artists are now influenced by the traditions of other cultures which show, although for different reasons, a similar concern. Examples of these range from child art to the sophisticated sculptures of Africa and South America.

## Abstract sculptures

Many modern sculptors are primarily concerned with the abstract qualities of their work. Sculptures which come into this category are those which are not dependent on a specific source but base their form on a general concept, which in turn results from the consideration of a number of separate instances. This type of work differs from the stylized sculptures previously discussed in that it communicates information about that which a number of objects have in common, as opposed to establishing their individual differences. The results of either process can appear very similar but it is important, particularly for the person working in this field, to distinguish between works which do not relate to any specific experience and works which retain visual evidence of the original object or situation on which they were based. Many people, even today, still find this type of art difficult to accept. This is usually due to a misunderstanding and will only be overcome if they can be persuaded to accept its essentially non-representational nature. There is of course a long tradition of abstract art in music and to a lesser extent in architecture, and quite often the very people who scorn abstract painting and sculpture are moved by these other abstract forms because they do not approach them with the same set of preconceptions. Abstract sculptures must be seen as objects existing in their own right, in such a way that they themselves become the image rather than the vehicles for other images. As we have seen in earlier chapters, the sculptor has always been concerned, in some way, with such abstract qualities as balance, contrasts, tension and rhythm. In purely abstract sculpture it is possible to deal exclusively with these interests.

When compared with other art forms, probably the most fundamental attribute of sculpture is its three-dimensional nature, that is its existence in real space. This interaction between sculpture and space can take three forms: the sculpture can occupy space, it can contain space, and it can also define an area of space. A simple box structure would serve to illustrate these possibilities. If it were closed in on all sides it would primarily occupy a definite area of space in relation to its size. If one of the sides could be opened it would then also demonstrate the enclosure of a cubic area of space, but if it was constructed in a linear way, with all the sides open, it would serve to distinguish between one area of space inside and the other area outside.

Most sculptures are of course much more complex than the simple box structure, but an understanding of this basic construction will help in appreciating their fundamental nature. In order to manipulate the abstract quality of their work, and to provide an element of discipline otherwise lacking, many sculptors use simple geometric forms in the construction of their work. This does not mean that the work is essentially of a mathematical nature but rather that, because these forms are universally recognized, they provide a method of direct constant communication.

Many people are misled by the superficial appearance of this type of work into thinking of it as too cold and calculated to afford them any satisfaction. While it is true that the actual making of these sculptures calls for this approach, I can assure them that the emotional stimulus responsible for the sculpture and the satisfaction that can be gained from communicating it is just as great as with the more traditional forms. The nature of art leads to a constant development first in one direction and then, like a pendulum, to the other. These developments, while always in some way related to a previous tradition, can appear to be revolutionary in their initial impact. Some of the recent and most exciting abstract sculptures have progressed beyond the stage of seeing the sculpture as a single self-possessed object and involve deliberate constructions which create a whole environment. In these works the active participation of the spectator, as he wanders under, round and through them, is an integral part of the whole work. Once again a new and sympathetic approach needs to be added to one's appreciation if these sculptures are to be fully enjoyed.

7

# Basic design

All sculpture of a figurative or representative nature, regardless of style, imposes a discipline on the artist by providing a selection of specific information which must be communicated by the successful sculpture. In all types of work, this information can be supplemented by more general observations but in the case of abstract work it is the general information alone which provides the artist with his source. In order to create abstract sculpture, the artist must provide himself, in the conception of each piece, with a discipline which is definite enough to enable him to evaluate the success or failure of his work. In addition to providing this necessary element of criticism, the careful choice of discipline can also stimulate the whole creative process.

This chapter is designed primarily for the person interested in taking up abstract sculpture, and the suggested exercises, which are concerned with some of the most fundamental aspects of sculpture, should provide a useful starting point. A knowledge of basic design, however, can be used as the grammatical base for the whole language of sculpture and the exercises should also be useful to all students, regardless of their personal inclinations. The suggested method of working can, of course, be extended beyond the immediate problems set by the initial projects, once the method of imposing creative restrictions is understood.

## An exercise with squares on a rectangular base

The first exercise involves the design of an abstract relief sculpture. The design is restricted to the use of squares on a rectangular base and should show a concern for balance, contrast and rhythm. The first restriction is imposed because a relief sculpture provides the easiest introduction to the fields of casting and armature-making. It also enables a simple two-dimensional drawing to be extended, in a relatively easy way, to a three-dimensional statement. The elements of the design are restricted to squares as these provide an easily recognized but unemotionally biased form. A similar design made up of roses could cause confusion because it would not be absolutely clear whether or not the impact of the work was due to the quality of the design or to the innate attractiveness of the subject. The choice of a rectangular base will provide, from the start, a related but slightly contrasting area to the squares.

Before starting the exercise, it is very important to recognize that full benefit will only be obtained if the final ideas result from a discovery of the many possibilities within the limited situation rather than from the imposing of a predetermined concept. This method calls for an open-minded use of the most obvious solutions in the early stages of the design so that even the most complex final sculpture is the result of a cumulative process. A series of purely experimental simple line drawings, dealing with each limitation in turn, should be used as a starting point. After some consideration, it should be possible to select a rectangle of fixed proportions which will be of either a horizontal or a vertical nature.

The general concept of balance suggests the idea of division, with one side balancing another. The rectangle can only be

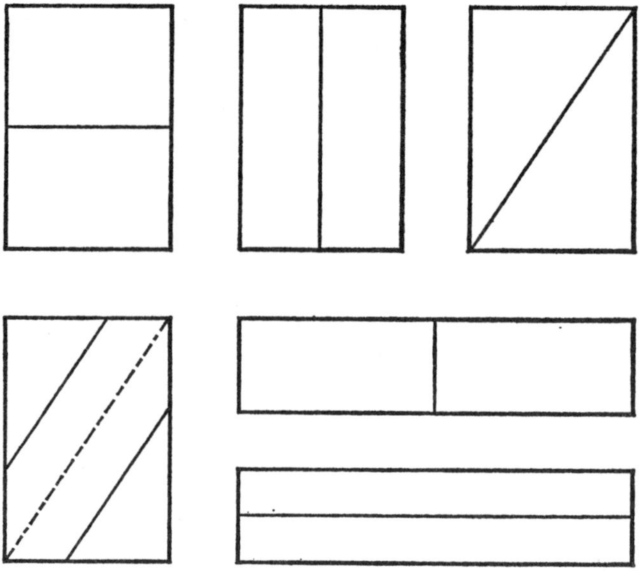

Figure 14 Dividing a rectangle

divided by using a vertical, horizontal or diagonal line as all other divisions are only more sophisticated variations of these basic three.

The element of contrast can also be considered at this stage because there is an opportunity to contrast the nature of the division with the nature of the rectangle. The use of this particular contrast is of course not obligatory because the squares will provide a much greater area of possible contrasts. Size is the most obvious of these variations and a great variety of compositions will result from the balancing of large and small squares. Another area of possible contrast is the disposition of the squares within the space of the rectangle. By changing their relationship with each other and with the angles of the rectangle it is possible to retain their structural character as

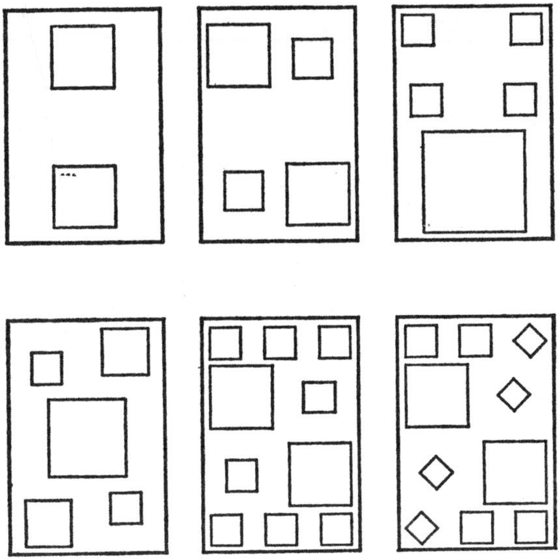

Figure 15 Contrast in size and relationship

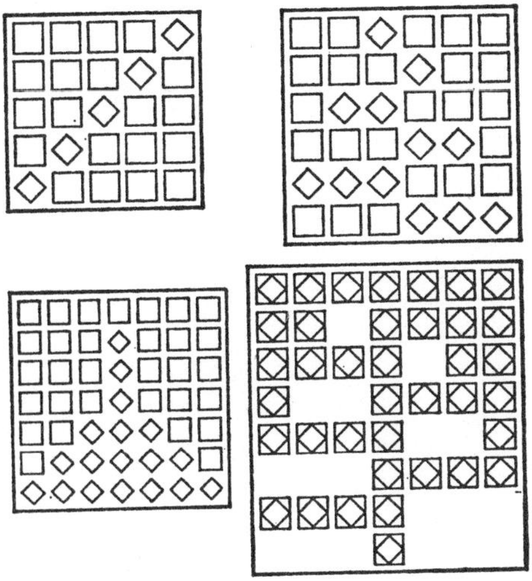

Figure 16 Some simple rhythms

squares but to change their appearance to that of a diamond. If this is used in conjunction with variations in size a further series of possible compositions will result.

To achieve the third requirement of rhythm it will be necessary to take the designs a stage further so that they set up a pattern of recurring shapes and spaces. This two-dimensional preparatory work should now have reached a stage where a successful design can be selected and developed into a three-dimensional statement. This involves the projection of parts of

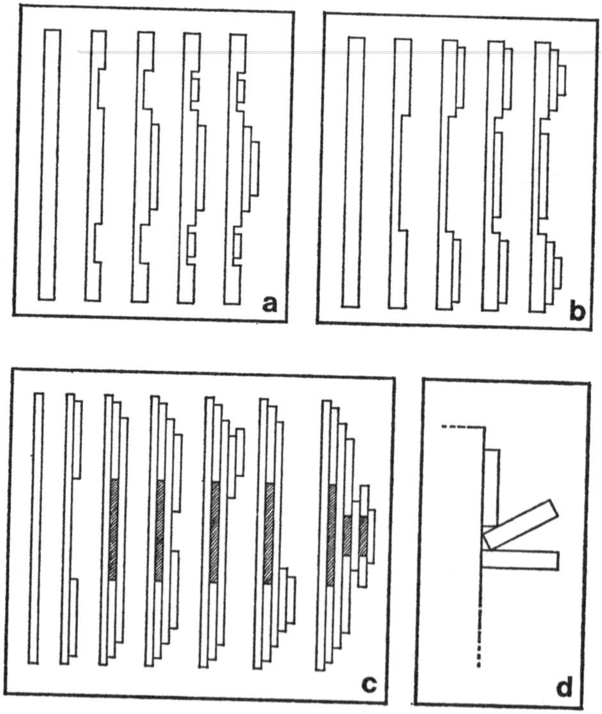


Figure 17 Diagram of some projections in relief: a and b, cutting into and building up on a clay bed; c, building with rigid materials; d, variations in the angle of projection

the design into real space. The amount of the projection will provide another area of possible contrast and should be related to the overall proportions and size of the chosen rectangle. This is not an area of precise specification but I would suggest that a projection limited to a maximum of two inches on a base of twenty-four inches would provide ample scope for exploring the design possibilities. The projection should be considered so that it provides a sympathetic comment on the original linear design. Further contrast and complementary rhythms can be established if the squares are projected at different angles to each other and the base.

The actual sculpture can be made by adding previously cut squares of clay to a clay bed of the selected rectangular form. If the clay bed is made one inch thicker than the proposed projection, further variations can be made by cutting down into the clay to the same depth as the projection. Efficient working on a design of this nature is made much easier if the clay has an even surface at the start of the modelling. This can be done quite easily by striking the surface level across two side battens of the required height. One great advantage of clay as a medium for sculpture is the fact that wholesale corrections can be made as the work progresses. By making full use of this facility the experimental nature of the design project can be continued up to a very late stage.

The use of texture and the precision of the design can be left to the discretion of the student but it is important that these do not interfere with the solutions to the original requirements. The necessary information for making a suitable armature and also for casting the finished work are given in the relevant chapters.

After the successful completion of the first sculpture, further experience can be gained by slightly changing the original requirements or by introducing more complex shapes. It is also a good idea to attempt the same project but on a fully three-dimensional as opposed to a relief basis as soon as the necessary technical skills are acquired.

## An exercise with spatial relationships

As the student progresses a further basic design exercise, dealing with the relationship of one object to another in space, will be useful. The form of this exercise makes it purely experimental, concerned solely with acquiring information, but the results can be incorporated into any subsequent sculpture.

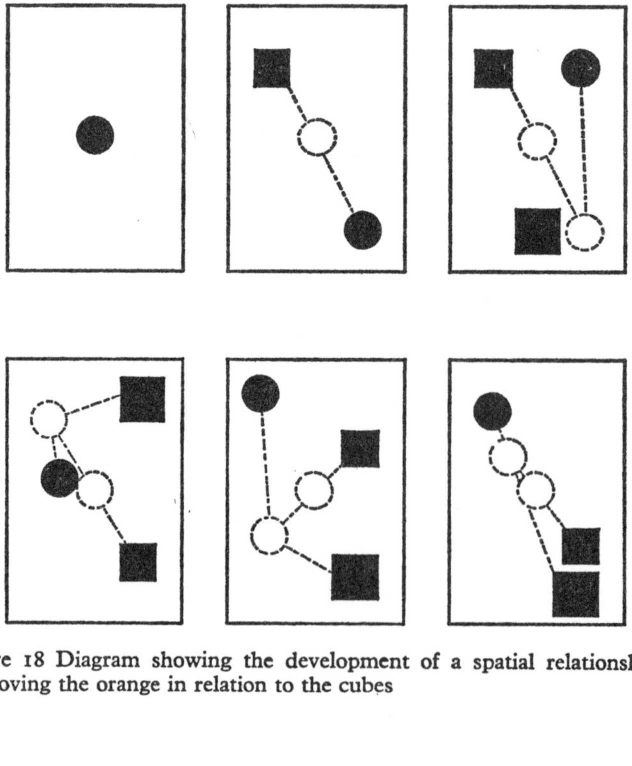

Figure 18 Diagram showing the development of a spatial relationship by moving the orange in relation to the cubes

The basic materials required are an orange, two blocks of wood of varying sizes but slightly larger than the orange, and a fair-sized rectangular board or plain table top.

At the start of each variation of this exercise, the orange is placed in the exact centre of the board so that it has a balanced and equal relationship with the whole of the chosen space. One of the blocks of wood is then placed on the board quite arbitrarily and the orange moved so that it achieves a relationship with both the block and the remaining area of space. The second block is then added and the orange again moved so that it includes the second block in its relationship with the whole situation. Arbitrary placing of the blocks allows this exercise to be repeated again and again, with each time the student making notes of how and why the orange has been moved. In each case the orange can be placed by eye so that it looks balanced, or the situation caused by the blocks can be evaluated and the orange placed so that it completes the composition. In the early exercises the orange, which is radically different from the other elements, serves to make the situation immediately apparent but similar exercises, using a greater number and variety of different objects, can be developed. These exercises extend and bring under control a faculty which we all use when arranging furniture or even laying a table.

## Exercises with colour

In most cultures, colour has traditionally been an important part of sculpture, although it was often used decoratively and made subservient to the form. In European sculpture, until comparatively recently, this area has been rather neglected, but the simple forms of so many abstract sculptures offer an opportunity for colour to play a vital part.

A reasonable knowledge of the variety of available colour,

and the behaviour of one colour in relation to another, are the prime requirements. There are quite a number of colour theories available but for the artist there can be no substitute for the actual emotional response to colour as part of his everyday life.

For the person with very little experience of using colour, a reasonable working knowledge can be fairly rapidly acquired by concentrating on one colour at a time. As many examples as possible of the chosen colour should be collected, from a wide variety of sources. This collection should then be arranged visually in a relevant order. In doing this it will be found that most of the variations are caused by the suggestion of other colours. If, for example, yellow had been selected as the colour to be researched, the available examples should vary from a yellow which is almost a green to another yellow which is almost an orange.

A further series of experiments will show that the character of one colour can be made either more or less apparent by changing the colour next to it. If we again use yellow as an example, and choose a yellow which is slightly green, it will be found that when placed next to a more powerful green, the green in the original choice will be cancelled out to make it appear more positively yellow. In the same way, if it is placed with an orange, the green element will, by contrast, become more apparent. By using information gained in this way, it is possible to compose colour combinations which have a controlled reaction.

It is also possible to distinguish between shades of colour which are caused by mixing colours together and tones of colour which are the result of increasing or decreasing the strength of a particular colour. This knowledge of colour in general can now be applied to the colouring of sculptures. It must always be used so that the colour is in some way sym-

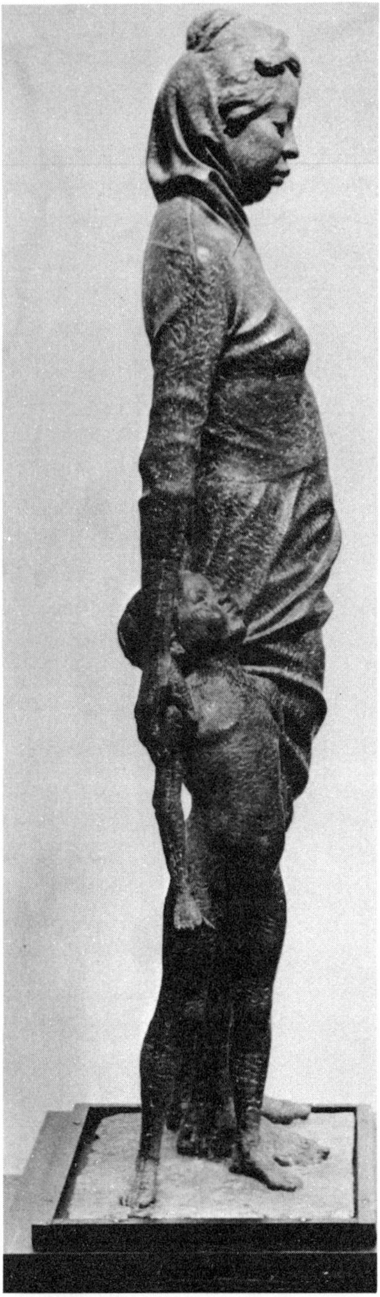

'Mother and Child' by Fay Simmons
*ciment fondu* 1963

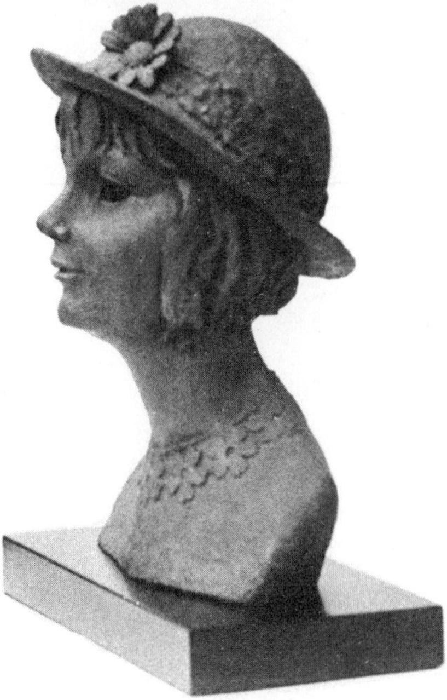

'Young Girl' by Fay Simmons
bronze 1970

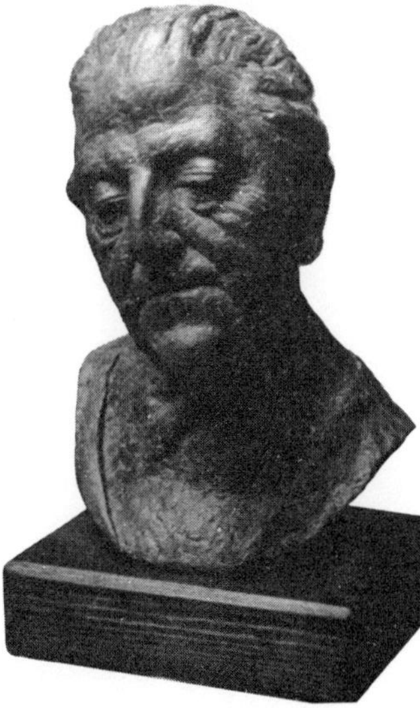

'Portrait' by Fay Simmons
*ciment fondu* 1962

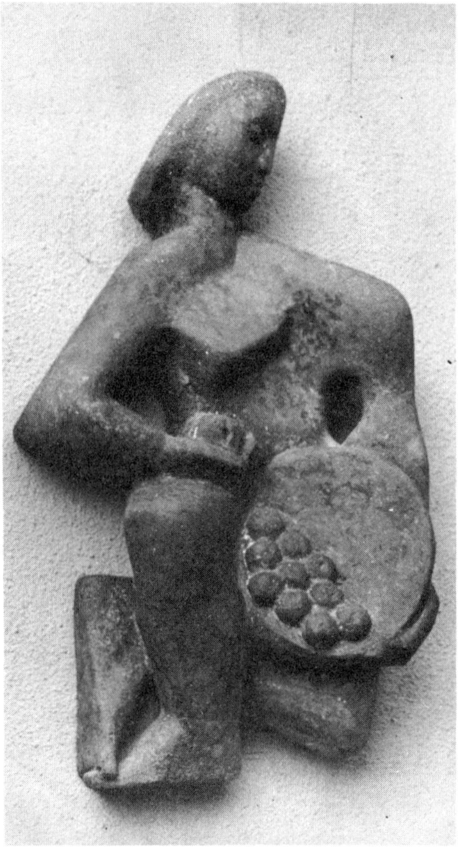

'Fertility Figure' by Sean Mullaney
coloured cement 1958

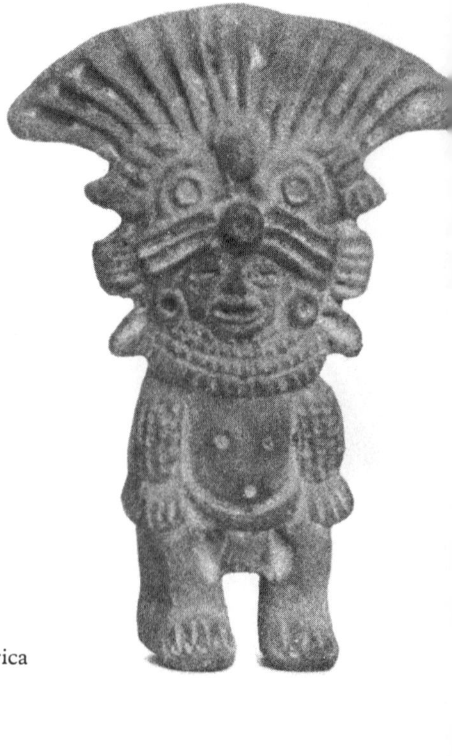

Small Terra Cotta
Pre-columbian America

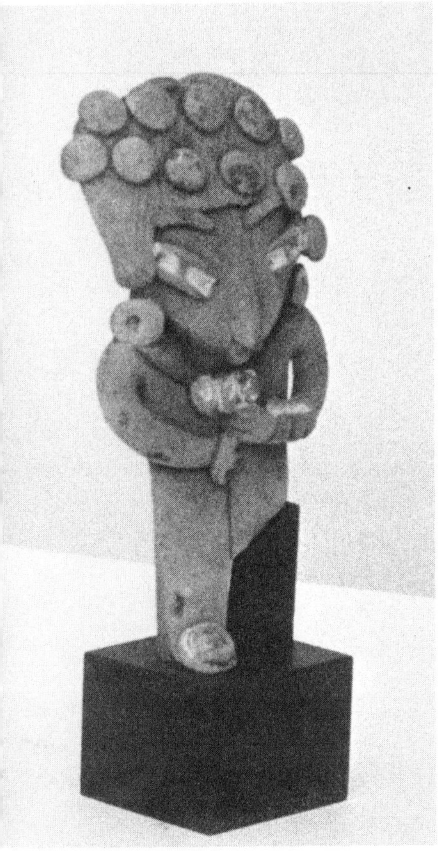

Pottery Figure
Mexico-Guana Juato before 1000 BC

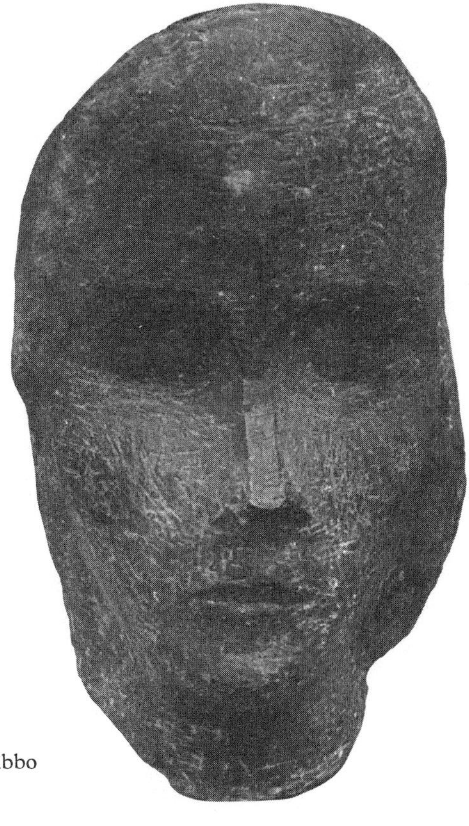

'Large Mask' by Jussuf Abbo
bronze 1920

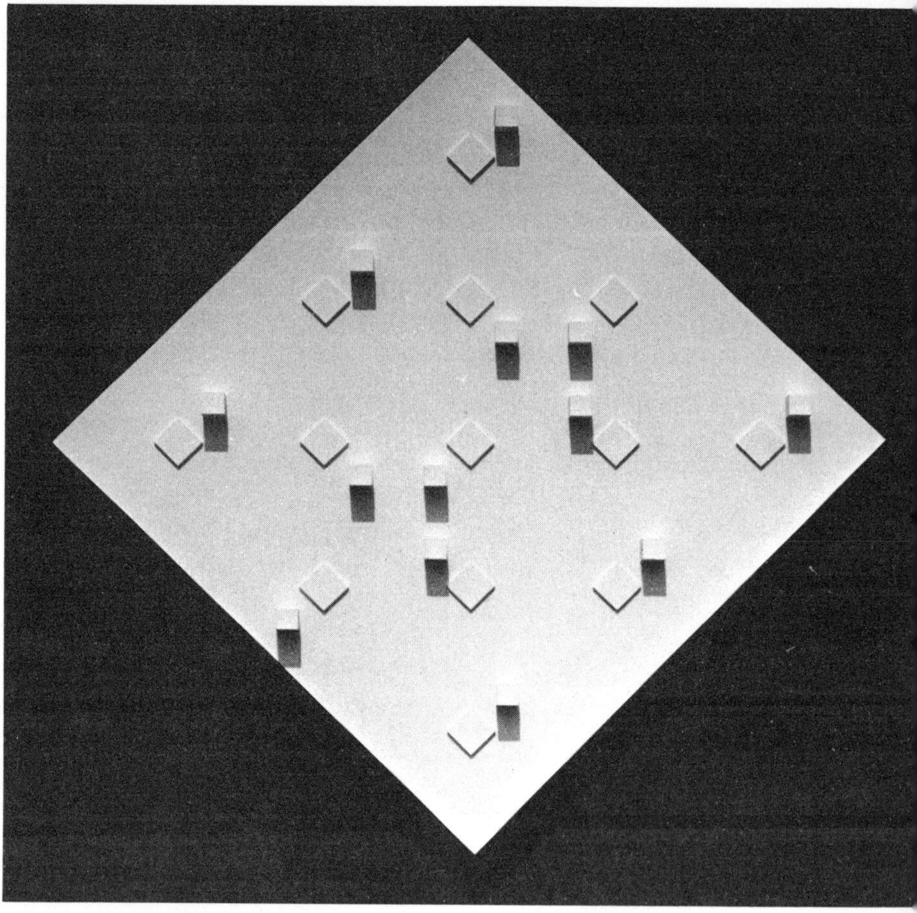

' White Relief ' by John Cross
painted wood 1970

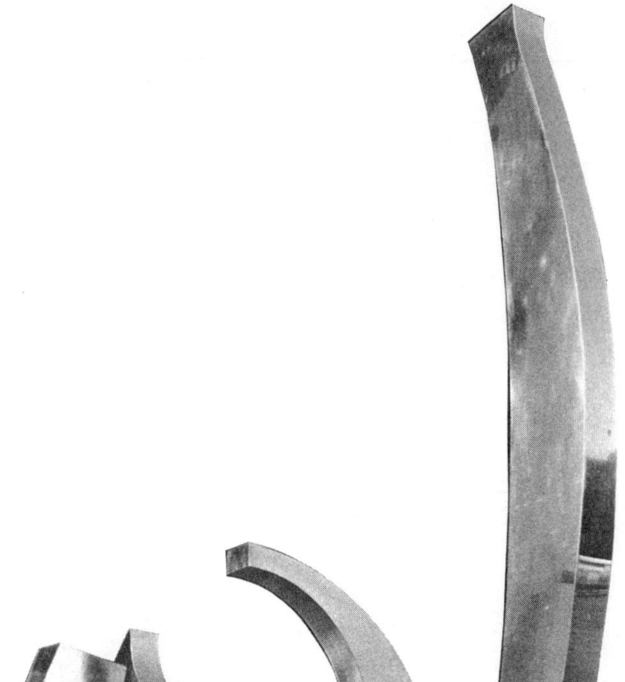

' Scorpio Major ' by Jesse Watkins
polished aluminium 1969

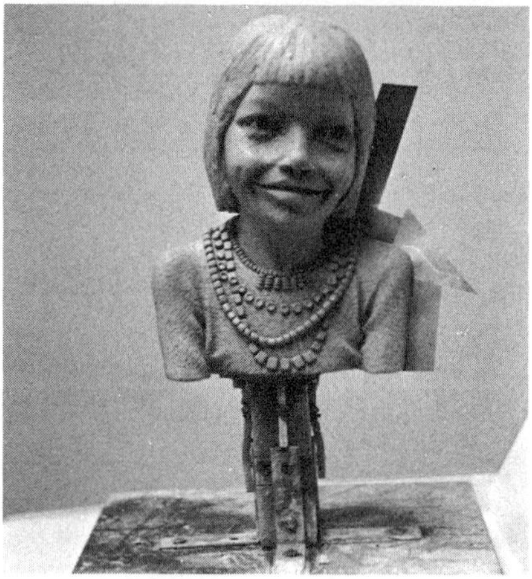

1 Putting in the brass fencing to divide the sections of the mould

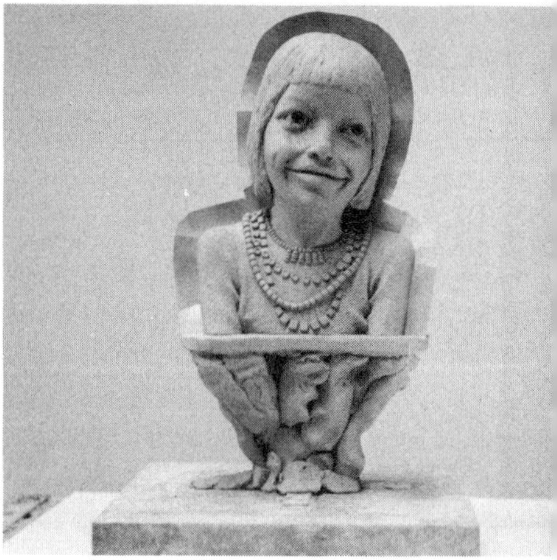

2 Brass fencing completed

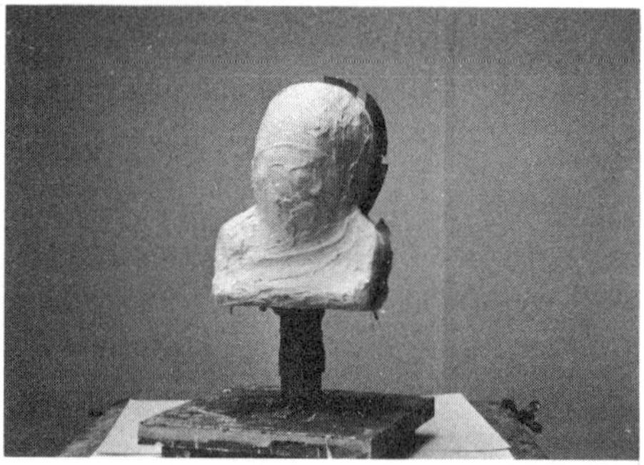

5 Taking out the brass fencing to separate the pieces of the mould

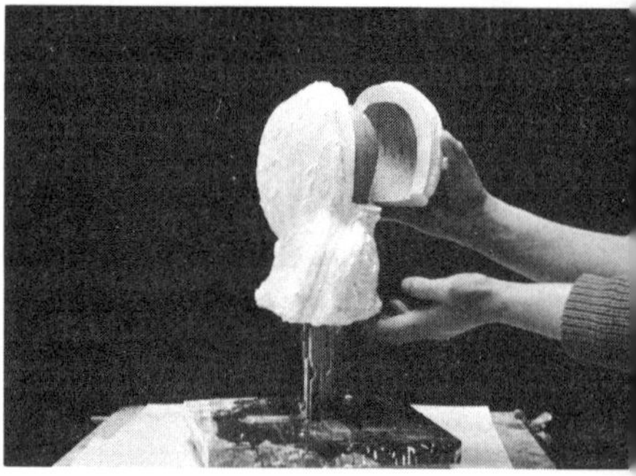

6 Removing the caps

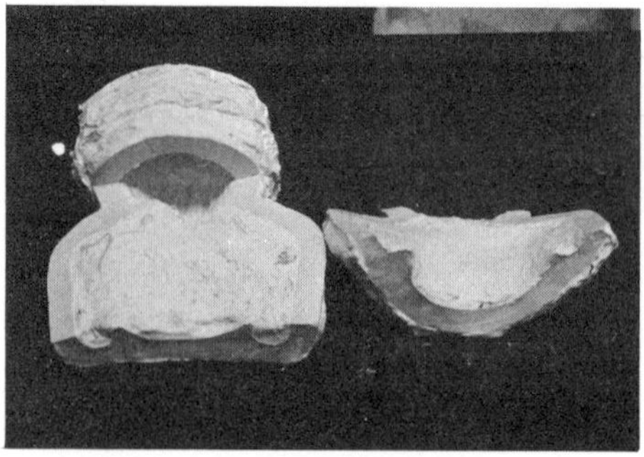

9 Separate pieces of the mould filled with plaster and scrim

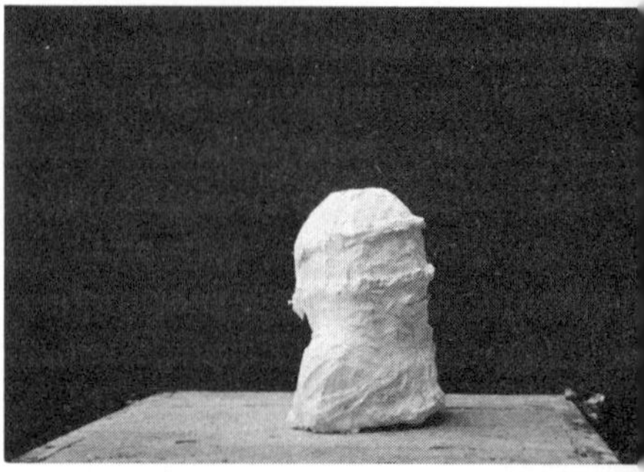

10 Filled mould reassembled with the seams sealed and the caps held in position by scrim bandages

STAGES IN THE CASTING PROCESS

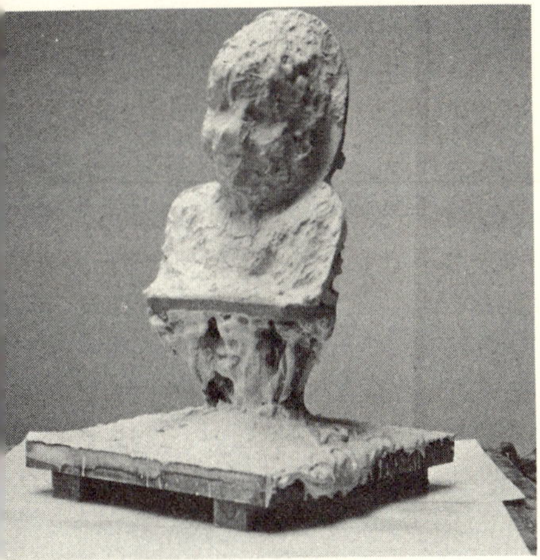

3 The first coat of plaster applied

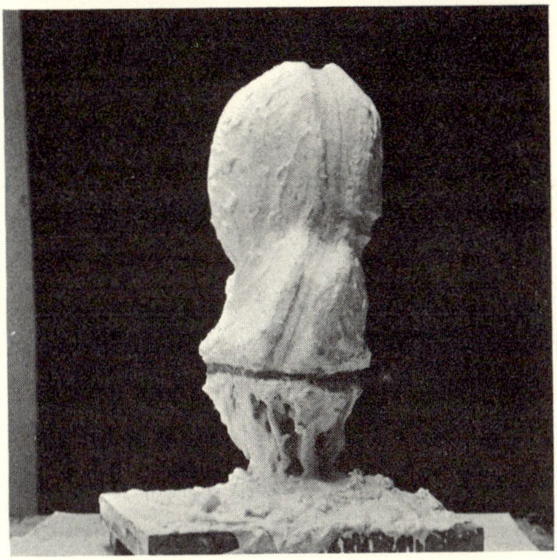

4 Plaster built up to the level of the brass fencing and a protective layer of scrim applied

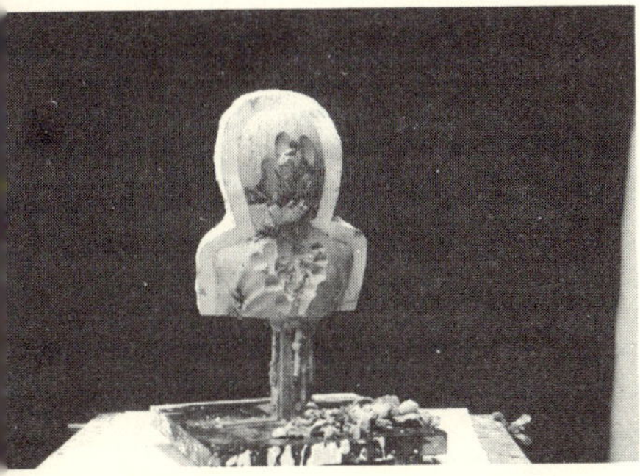

7 Digging out the clay from the mother mould

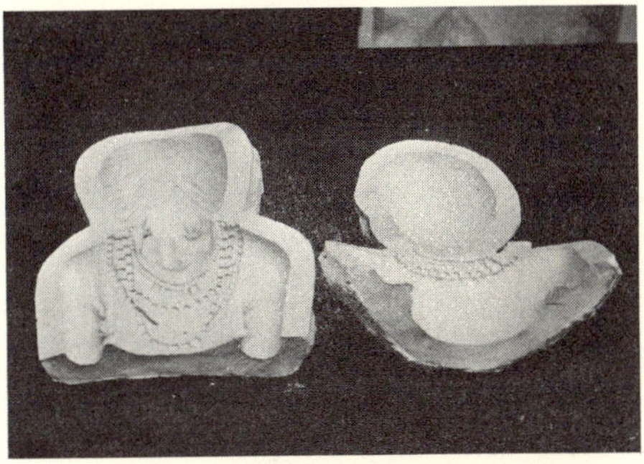

8 Clay removed and the mould washed and soft soaped ready for filling

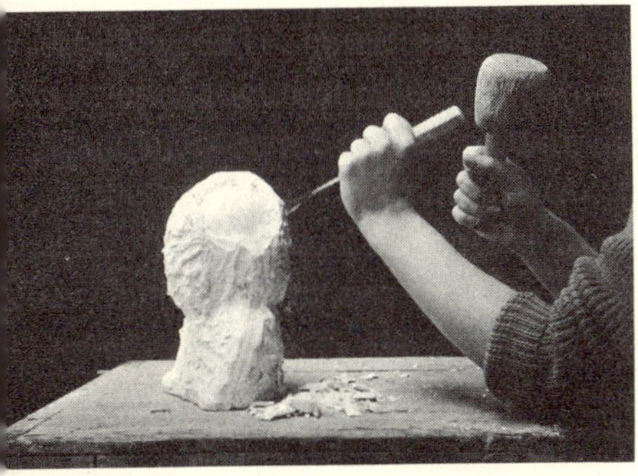

11 Starting to chip out the cast

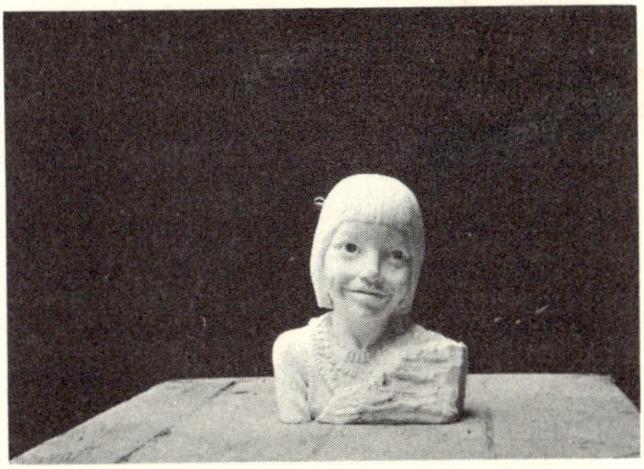

12 The plaster cast almost chipped out

STAGES IN THE CASTING PROCESS

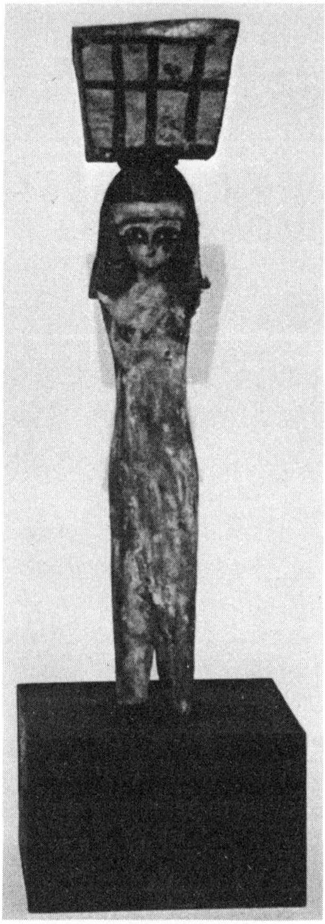

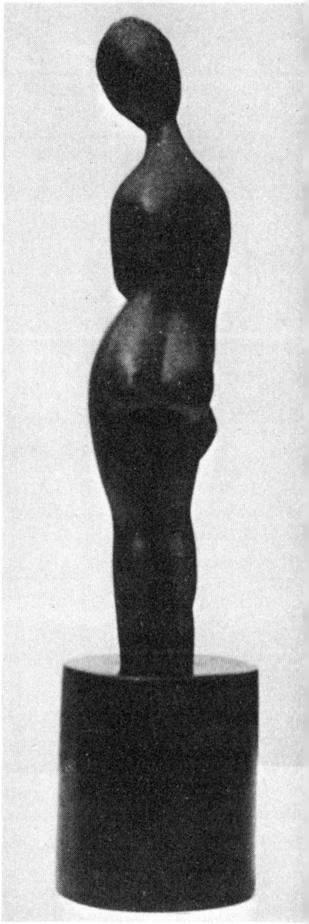

' Small Figure '
by Moissey Kogan
bronze 1930

Egyptian Figure of a Servant
painted wood Eleventh Dynasty

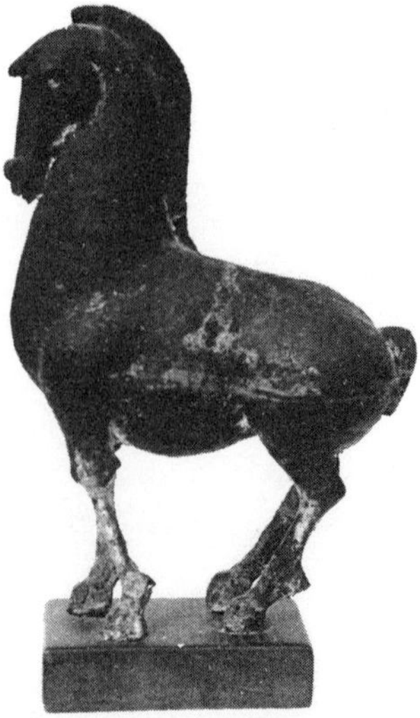

' Horse ' by Sean Mullaney
*ciment fondu* 1960

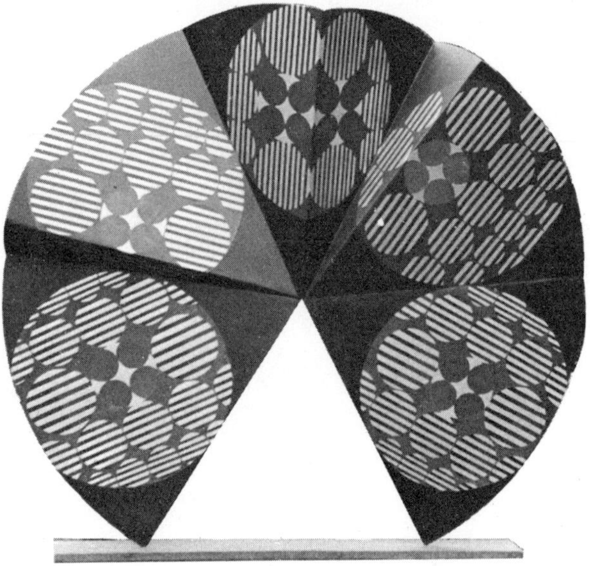

' Gold on Painted Wood ' by Sean Mullaney
construction 1966

' To the Place that's Best ' by Michael Cady
painted wood 1970

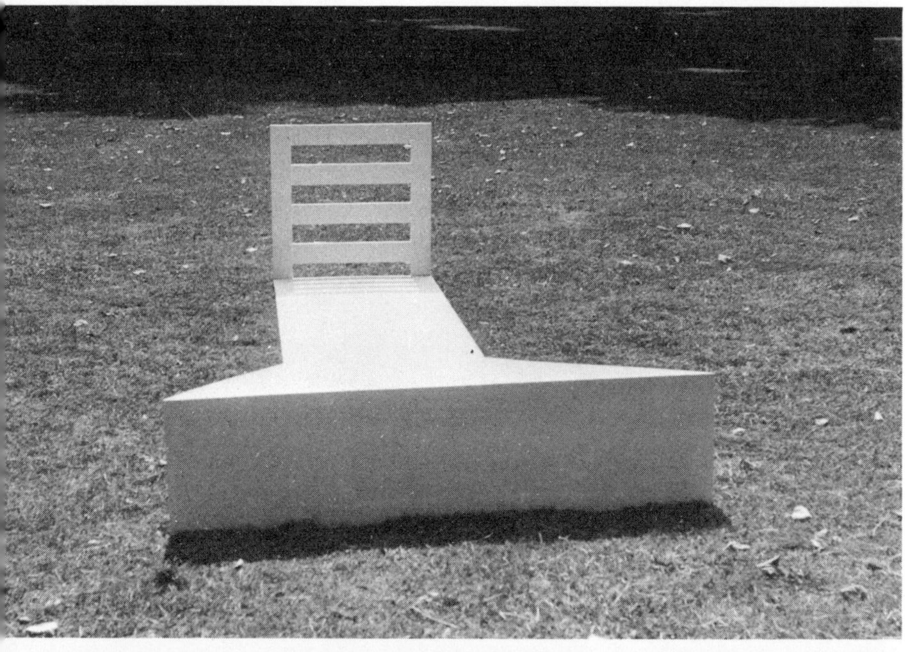

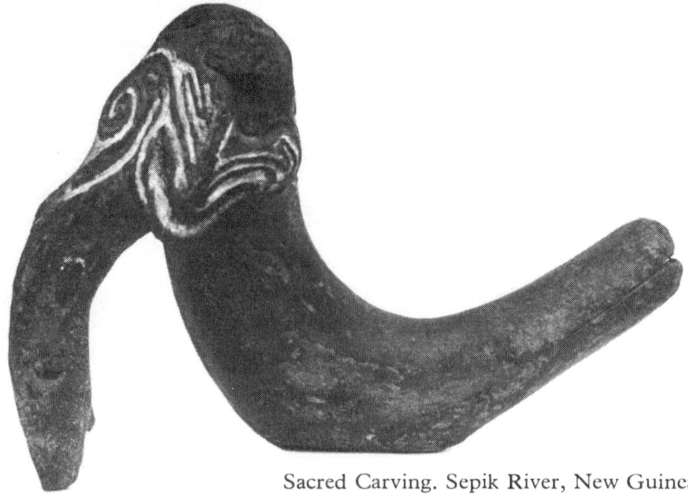

Sacred Carving. Sepik River, New Guinea
wood

'Equilibrium' ('Lola's Tangent') by Tom Sim
enamelled wood 1970

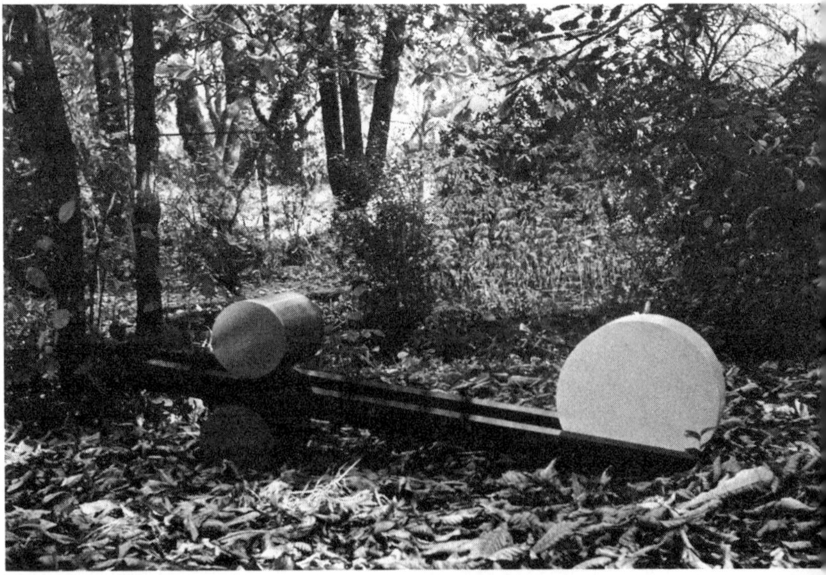

pathetic to the design, either by complementing or by contrasting the form. At first it will be easier if only one colour is used for each sculpture. In this way, for example, a delicate pale colour could, by contrast, emphasize the boldness of a particular composition, or the impact of the whole work could be increased by the use of an equally bold colour.

The following exercise is designed to show how changes in colour radically affect the character of individual sculptures. First it is necessary to produce a fairly large quantity of identical simple constructions so that the effects of different colours on the same form can be evaluated. The effect of different colours in the immediate environment on the colour of an object can also be studied, using the same constructions. When more than one colour is used in a sculpture, the interaction of the colour as well as their effect on the form must be considered. The same set of constructions can again be used to explore these possibilities if a series of deliberate step-by-step changes are made in the design and a considered change of colour used to comment on each change as it occurs.

The final and most complex way of using colour is to set up, on the sculpture, a painted design which is related but not identical to the formal design of the work. A series of experiments in which curved areas of colour are set against straight areas of form, and vice versa, will provide an introduction to using colour in this way.

8

# Construction and assemblage

## Construction: wood, metal and plastic

Construction is primarily a technique for making sculptures, but because of the close interaction between material, method and intention, it can also influence the nature of any sculpture to which it is applied. If, for example, the first basic design exercise described in the previous chapter was constructed out of metal, perspex or wood instead of clay, even though the requirements remained the same, the work would have a radically different character, due to the nature and appearance of each of the different materials. With metals the opportunities for polishing and etching and the effect of these on the design would have to be considered. The translucence of perspex would be bound to provide a great number of possible variations, while the natural colour and grain of wood offers a chance of increased subtlety. The common constructional nature of these materials would also suggest the possibility of using them in combination.

Construction differs from the more traditional techniques of sculpture in that it consists of joining together previously shaped pieces of material to form the sculpture, as opposed to manipulating a mass of material into the desired shape. It is particularly suitable for abstract sculpture, where the simplicity of the basic forms is complemented by the directness of the technique. Sculptures made in this way enable the design to be translated directly into a permanent material and allow the sculptor with only a modest amount of equipment to work on fairly large pieces.

These advantages are, for some sculptors, counteracted by the comparatively inflexible nature of the method. Unlike clay, which is so malleable, the materials of construction call for a design which has previously been worked out in some detail. It is essential, for efficient working in this technique, that the maquette or working model is in a material of a similar character to the proposed sculpture.

In addition to the traditional craft techniques associated with the materials of construction, the sculptor can use with advantage many of the modern adhesives and bonding agents. These are too numerous to describe in detail but I would advise the student to read the manufacturers' instructions for each product very carefully as with many of these it is the precision of application which is responsible for their strength.

Wood is probably the most popular material used in construction. It is comparatively cheap and generally available in a great variety of sizes and types. If properly seasoned and protected it can be used for sculptures which are to be exhibited out of doors. Providing the first designs are not too ambitious, constructions can be made in wood by methods which do not unduly tax the craftsmanship of the sculptor. This should strongly recommend it to the person taking up construction, as it is always more satisfying if the development of technical ability can be achieved as part of the whole creative process.

### Constructions in welded metal

Welded metal constructions, for which mild steel is the most popular material, enable the sculptor to produce works of a very strong durable nature. The traditional technique of join-

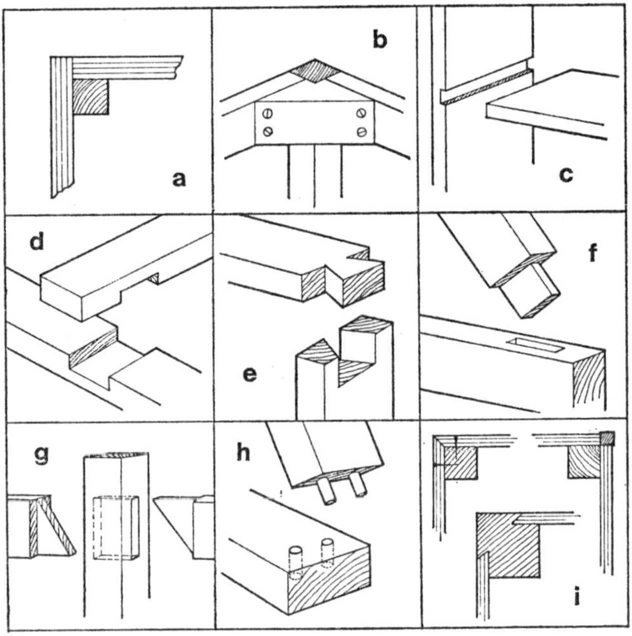


Figure 19 Some useful wood joints:
a, butt joint; b, angle bracket; c, housed joint; d, halved joint; e, dovetail joint; f, mortise and tenon; g, mortise and tenon for fencing; h, dowelled joint; i, joints suitable for plywood

ing pieces of metal together by welding, however, does call for a definite degree of craftsmanship and involves the use of specialized equipment. This can be dangerous if carelessly or improperly handled and the person taking up this craft will need some direct personal tuition.

In essence, welding consists of joining two pieces of the same material by fusing them together while they are in a molten state. The craftsmanship lies in controlling the heat in the right place and then gradually moving a bead of molten metal along the join so that the weld has an even maximum strength. In most cases oxyacetylene rather than electric arc welding is used in sculpture. The manufacturers of the necessary equipment will advise the sculptor on the setting up and running of a suitable workshop. They also run special courses dealing with the welding of difficult materials such as aluminium.

Instructions for forming and bonding the many different and attractive plastics suitable for use in sculpture constructions are willingly supplied by the manufacturers or their retailers. The very attractiveness of these materials, however, especially the coloured varieties, can be a disadvantage unless carefully controlled. The artist must impose a definite though sensitive formal element in his design if their immense sculptural potential is going to be fully realized. It will help him to avoid superficial work if he remembers that the credit for the intrinsic decorative appeal of these materials is largely due to the manufacturer.

Constructed sculptures, by their nature, go particularly well with the better examples of modern architecture and can be shown off to advantage in most urban settings. They can also be used to make an exciting contrast in more traditional situations. An area which the person taking up this type of work could usefully explore is play and garden sculpture. The extra discipline imposed by the functional requirements, coupled with the constructional nature of the traditional forms involved, can be quite easily and usefully combined with the purely artistic requirements. If looked at in the right way, the sculptural nature of such things as swings, slides, roundabouts and climbing frames will become immediately apparent.

## Assemblage

Assemblage is a fairly modern approach to the sculptor's

traditional concern for the making of images. The methods and techniques are similar to those described for construction and again the sculpture is made by joining together previously formed pieces. In assemblage, however, these items, which are often of a mass-produced nature, already possess a definite character. The wealth of material and possible images this makes available results in a very individualistic art form, which accommodates artists with a wide range of different concerns. The individual character of any object can be used to comment on the nature of a related or absurdly different image. Assemblage of large numbers of objects normally seen in isolation or different surroundings can emphasize or reveal an overlooked but intrinsic character of the object or the image.

The use of reproduction moulds, as well as making convenient the production of large numbers of objects, also enables the artist to comment on the nature of the original object by retaining the shape but changing the material. Assemblage demonstrates that a re-evaluation is necessary when any object is removed from its accepted environment. It enables the artist to comment directly on the society in which he lives, often by using objects that society ignores, takes for granted or discards.

9

# Plaster casting (the waste mould method)

## Moulding and casting

Sculptures originally modelled in clay must be transferred into a more permanent material because although clay is a very versatile medium it is too fragile to be suitable for a finished work. The method by which this transfer is usually made is known as the casting process, and is such a traditional part of sculpture that most artists consider the clay model to be only a stage in the progress towards their final work. This is an attitude which I would like to encourage because a considerable amount of time, skill and patience is required and if the casting is approached in a creative spirit it will prevent it from becoming an unpleasant chore.

The two main items involved in this process are the mould, which is a negative impression of the original work, and the cast which is taken from this mould, and which should be a perfect reproduction of the clay model.

A mould can be taken by any soft material which is later allowed to harden. A primitive version found in everyday life is the impression left by a footprint in muddy soil. In fact sometimes in detection work a cast is actually taken from this type of simple mould. In sculpture the mould is made by using a very fine plaster of paris, which if applied skilfully is quite capable of registering even the lightest finger-print on the original modelling. A variety of materials can be used to take a cast from a plaster mould but in this chapter I would like to describe the method by which a plaster cast is made by what is known as the waste mould method. This term is used because during the process the mould is broken up, which means that only one copy of the original model can be produced.

No extra tools or equipment need to be added to the basic range described in chapter 2 but it is advisable to make sure that both pairs of scissors, a knife, pliers and at least two polythene bowls are clean and readily available. Other materials used in this process are: thin gauge brass fencing, a fine grade of plaster of paris, plasterers' scrim (which is coarsely woven hessian), a little yellow powder colour, and soft soap, which is used as the separator. The sculptor must always remain aware that casting is a skilled process which calls for a high degree of craftsmanship. The complexity of this process can, however,

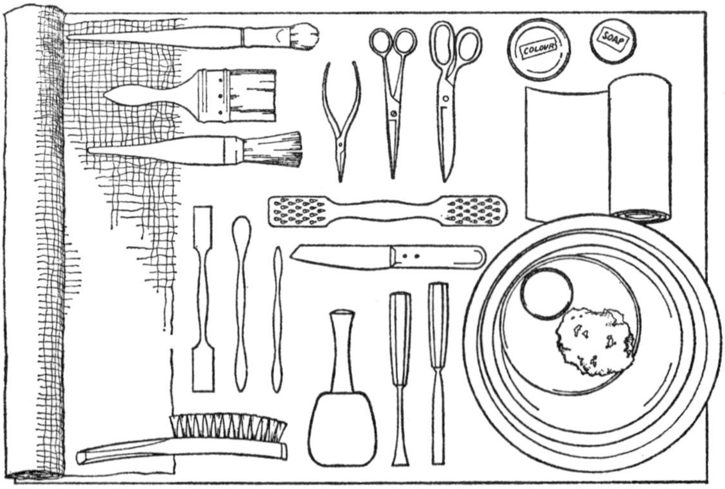


Figure 20 Plaster casting tools and materials

be reduced by concentrating exclusively on each stage as it is dealt with. Most mistakes are the result of carelessness or caused through trying to complete the work too quickly. Casting should always be left until it can be approached in a relaxed manner with ample time available.

## Designing the mould

The first stage in casting a sculpture is to design a suitable mould for the particular work which is to be cast. This means deciding on the number of pieces into which the mould will have to be divided so that the clay and armature can be easily removed, and to provide access for filling to all parts. Most simple sculptures, such as a torso or portrait head, can be cast in a two-piece mould, but with larger or more intricate sculptures the mould will have to be divided into a greater number of sections.

I would recommend the following method for all sculptures regardless of the number of pieces it is proposed to use. A series of lines, which indicate how the mould is to be divided, are first lightly drawn on the surface of the clay model, using a sharp knife. The first line should divide the sculpture vertically into two slightly unequal parts. The larger part is normally the front of the sculpture or the area with the greatest amount of detailed modelling. The section of the mould which will encase this larger part is popularly known as the mother mould and the smaller piece is referred to as a cap. This back cap can be further divided into a series of sections for ease of handling or if the sculpture contains a potentially weak form, such as the neck on a portrait bust. If there are forms on the front of the sculpture which will not allow access from the back, further caps can be taken from the mother mould but these must be designed as separate pieces so that the main

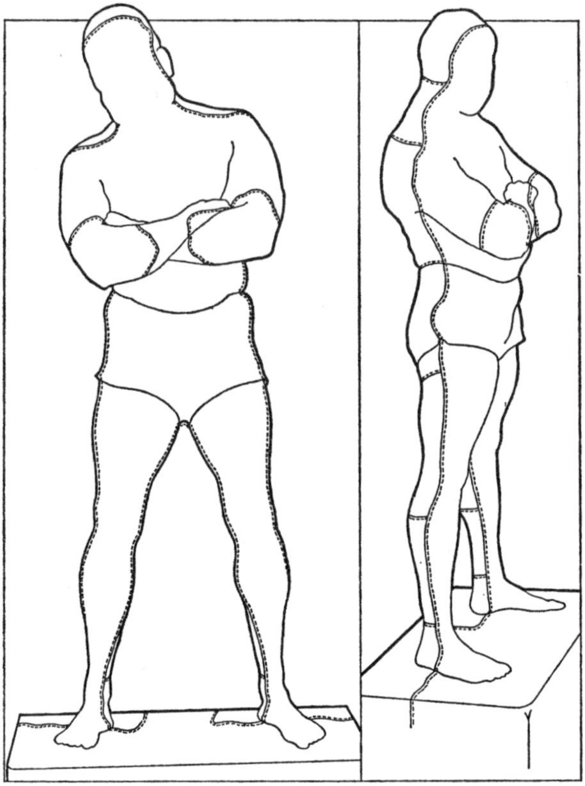

Figure 21 Diagram of the dividing lines for casting a life size sculpture

section of the mould remains one complete piece.

Designing the mould is probably the most difficult part of casting because it necessitates imagining what the work will look like in later stages. This is why it is always better to start by casting a simple sculpture and so gradually gain experience.

## Dividing the mould

The lines which divide the sculpture are known as seams and

wherever possible these should be drawn on the high points of the form so that the inevitable marks can be more easily removed from the finished cast. There are two methods which can be used to achieve the actual division of the mould; one involves the use of a clay wall to separate the sections, while the other uses thin brass fencing to obtain the same effect. The clay wall method is probably easier for the beginner but is only suitable for simple two-or-three-piece moulds. The brass fencing method is suitable for all moulds, including the very complex.

When the clay wall is used the separation is made by rolling out a sheet of fairly stiff clay to a thickness of approximately one-quarter of an inch. This is then cut into strips the width of which will determine the final thickness of the mould. This will vary depending on the size of the sculpture involved but is usually between three-quarters of an inch to two inches maximum. When the strips have been cut to the required width they are laid edge-on to the model, following the marked line and fitting tightly to the contours of the form. They can be cut into as many lengths as are necessary to achieve a good fit but they must be joined together once they are applied to the sculpture. With this method each section is cast separately and the mother mould is usually dealt with the first. The surface of the clay wall facing the section to be cast must be kept as smooth as possible while the back is reinforced with extra coils of clay.

The brass fencing, which is used as an alternative separator, is normally supplied in rolls six inches wide, and is sold by weight. Various thicknesses are available, .003 gauge being a good general-purpose size. The brass should always be cut across the width of the roll to give strips six inches long. The width of the strips will again vary depending on the size of the sculpture but they should be between one inch and two and one-quarter inch maximum. With both methods care should be taken to keep the thickness of the mould as uniform as possible to prevent possible weaknesses and to avoid the danger of warping. The strips of brass can be cut up into smaller pieces for ease of handling and are inserted into the clay model along the dividing line to the depth of about one-quarter of an inch. By cutting pieces at an angle it is possible to follow the contours of the sculpture exactly and still maintain an even thickness. Care must be taken when cutting the brasses to avoid ragged sharp edges.

The advantage of the brass fencing method is that the brass is left in to become the separation and so the whole of the mould can be cast at the same time. With a clay wall each section is cast in turn, the wall is removed after the first section

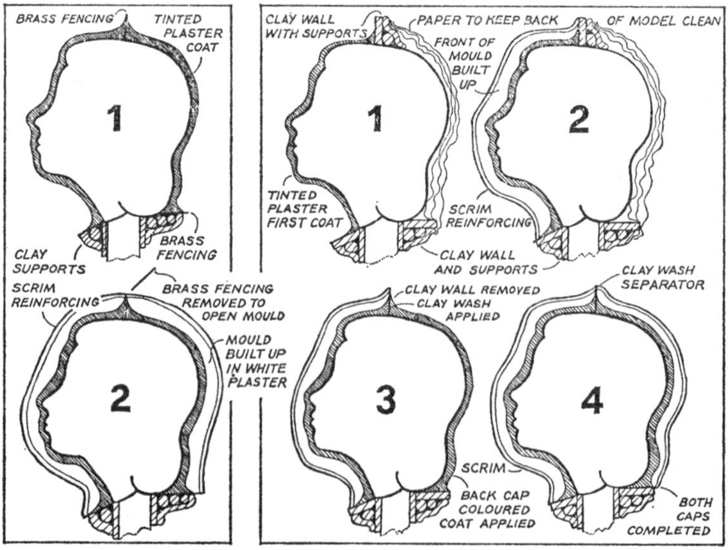


Figure 22 Diagram showing the use of a clay wall and brass fencing

is completed and the resultant seam coated with a thin wash of clay and water to prevent it from sticking to the second section. The second section is then treated in the same way if the mould is designed to be in three pieces.

## Applying the plaster

Applying the plaster to the model is a messy business and so it is advisable to protect the general casting area with sheets of polythene. It is also important to wear an overall or old clothes because during casting the first concern must be the sculpture and any thought of one's appearance would be a miserable distraction.

During the various stages of this process it will be necessary to use plaster of different consistencies, but, regardless of the working consistency required, the plaster is always mixed in the same way using the same proportions. The relative thickness is determined by how long it is allowed to stand after it has been mixed and under no circumstances should more plaster be added to the water, even if a thicker consistency is required.

In sculpture a fine-grade plaster should always be used. It must be carefully stored to protect it from damp, and any plaster which contains hard lumps must not be used for casting, as this could lead to loss of detail. If it has been stored for any length of time, plaster tends to pack down tightly and it must be gently agitated by hand until it feels light and aerated. When handling unmixed plaster, great care should be taken to make sure that both hands and containers are absolutely dry. I always keep a plentiful supply of paper towels available during the whole process.

Plaster is activated by mixing with water. Repeatedly successful mixes will be achieved by sprinkling the dry powder evenly into a shallow bowl until a thin coat of powder remains on the surface of the water. The amount of water used will depend on the amount of plaster required but in casting a series of small mixes is always preferable to one large one and under no circumstances should the bowl be more than half-full of water. The solution should not be stirred whilst the dry plaster is being added but when the correct proportion of mix has been achieved a smooth consistency can be obtained by agitating the solution with the palm of the hand pressed firmly against the bottom of the bowl.

When casting plaster to plaster in a waste mould the first coat is slightly tinted to help in recognition during the later stages. A little yellow ochre powder colour is added to the water in the early mixes. Only a very small quantity should be used as too much colour could weaken the plaster.

The first coat is applied to the model soon after the plaster has been mixed, while it is still fairly liquid, so that all the detail of the sculpture wil be registered in the mould. This coat is applied by flicking the liquid plaster vigorously against the clay model, starting at the bottom and gradually working up to the top. This method prevents the plaster from running down the figure and failing to penetrate all the undercuts. In places where there is considerable undercutting, such as the eyes and nostrils, it is advisable to make sure that the plaster has penetrated by blowing it into them as soon as it has been applied. The first coat should be built up, in this way, to an overall thickness of at least one-quarter of an inch, including the sides of the brass fencing or clay wall. This first coat should be left with a slightly rough texture so that it will key successfully to the second coat.

The second and subsequent coats are applied to build up the thickness of the mould to the size previously determined by the separating walls. This can be controlled more easily if the plaster is allowed to set to a paste-like consistency before it is used. At this stage the cast can be handled safely because the first coat will already be hard enough to protect the model. For this reason a minimum of two separate mixes are used even with very small sculptures.

When the mould has been built up to the required thickness, and if the clay wall method has been used, the wall can be removed and the clay wash separator applied before the process is repeated to cast the second section. If the mould has been divided by brass fencing the whole sculpture should now be encased. A sharp knife is used to scrape the area around the seams so that the thin top edge of the brass can be clearly seen. This will be much easier if at no stage the brass edge has been completely covered by the plaster. Each section of the mould can now be further strengthened with a layer of scrim dipped in plaster. Care must be taken to make sure that this scrim coat does not overlap the seams, as this would prevent the mould from being opened. If the mould is not likely to be subject to a great deal of stress a thin clay wash can be applied before the scrim coat is added. This will make the chipping-out of the final cast much easier.

When casting very large sculptures, or if there are delicate forms projecting from the main mass, the mould can be further strengthened by the addition of reinforcing irons made from square section mild steel rod. These must be sealed to prevent them from rusting and they are then placed in position directly on top of the first coat.

Moulds are usually easier to fill when lying down, and if necessary a constructed wooden cage can be attached to the scrim coat. This will of course add strength to the mould as well as making it more stable. If possible, the whole of the mould-making procedure should be carried out as a continuous process to prevent the clay from cracking or shrinking before

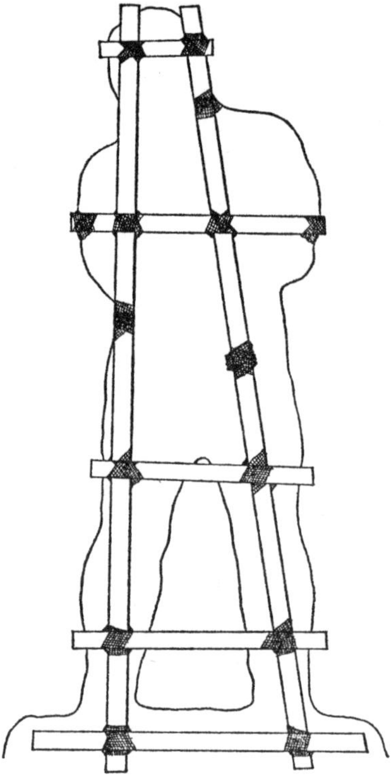

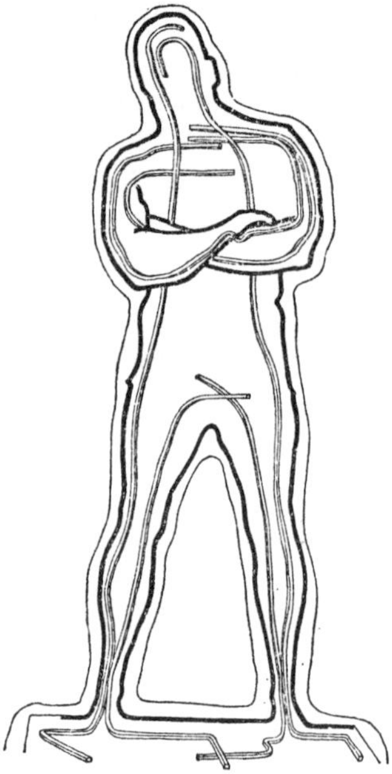

Figure 23 Life size mould supported by a wooden cage
Figure 24 Diagram of the reinforcing irons in a life size cast

the mould is completed. If there are unavoidable time lapses in the process, and one coat of plaster has been allowed to completely harden, then it must be dampened before the next coat is applied.

## The completed mould

The completed mould should be left to cure overnight before

the various sections are taken apart. If a clay wall has been used, the mould should be soaked in water until the caps can be pulled away easily. With brass fencing the mould can be opened more easily if the strips of brass are first carefully removed, using thin-nosed pliers. Water is then poured into the resultant gap to break the suction between the plaster mould and the clay mould. With either method a great deal of force should never be used; sufficient soaking will prevent this from being necessary. As the caps are removed they should be washed and carefully stored, preferably on end or inverted to prevent the possibility of warping. When all the caps have been separated, the clay and armature should be carefully removed from the mould. The mother mould must never be pulled away from the model as this could lead to loss of detail. As soon as the mould is cleaned, or if there is to be any lengthy interruption during the cleaning, all the caps must be tied firmly back into position.

## Filling the mould

The mould is now ready for filling and must be treated with the appropriate separator for a plaster cast. Soft soap is diluted in warm water and brushed gently into the dry mould. A lather will gradually form and when this covers the surface it should be left to soak in for about fifteen minutes. The mould is then washed under clean running water before more soap is applied. Two or three applications of soft soap are usually sufficient but the process should be continued until the washed mould surface feels slightly slippery to the touch. When used to make a plaster cast the mould must be thoroughly saturated before it is filled. It should be soaked until air bubbles cease to come to the surface of the water and then the surplus water drained or lightly sponged from the mould surface. Some sculptors then use a fine film of oil as an additional separator but this must always be as fine as possible, because excess oil, if it penetrated into the filling, could ruin the finished cast.

Each section of the mould is filled and allowed to set separately, before the pieces are reassembled. It is advisable to leave the ones not being worked on to soak until it is their turn to be filled. The plaster is used for filling in a very similar way to its use in the making of the mould. Once again the first coat is used whilst it is still fairly liquid because again it is the one which is going to take the impression of the sculpture. The plaster is mixed and applied in the same way but this time there is no need for the addition of a colouring agent to the water. This first coat should cover the surface, including any textured areas, to a depth of at least one-quarter of an inch. Scrim dipped in plaster is used with the second and subsequent coats as a reinforcing agent, but this time, as all the strength possible is needed, a clay wash must not be used. The seams must be kept absolutely clean during this process, a bowl of water and some small pieces of sponge enabling this to be done as the work progresses.

When dealing with large sculptures, or with a composition which has weak points, such as an arm projecting from the body or where the weight is taken on thin ankles, it is necessary to provide extra reinforcement. Mild steel square section rods are bent into shape and placed so that the weight is more evenly distributed throughout the mass. Two or more rods must be used together because a single rod acting as a pivot would weaken rather than strengthen the cast. The mild steel must be protected against rusting by a coating of brunswick black or a resin based sealer. Great care must be taken when fixing these supports so that they do not interfere with the correct assembling of the sections of the mould.

The method of joining the various sections of the cast together varies slightly depending on the size of a particular work. With sculptures which are small enough to be easily handled, the filled pieces are secured firmly together and the seams sealed with plaster and scrim. Liquid plaster is then poured into the mould until it is about one-third filled. The mould is then swung about in such a way that a coat of plaster is deposited on the whole of the inner surface before the surplus plaster is poured out. Using the same mix, this process is repeated two or three times and as each time the plaster will be a little thicker it will leave a greater amount inside the mould. A second mix of plaster is then used with scrim to reinforce the inside seams or, in the case of very small sculptures, to fill the cast solid. Just before the plaster sets the base can be struck level, using a metal rule or similar tool.

The second method of filling, which is suitable for all sculptures except the exceedingly small, involves the separate fixing of each section in turn. First, if any caps have been taken off the mother mould they are fixed and secured in position by a scrim and plaster bandage and the outside seams effectively sealed. The inside join is then achieved by a coat of liquid plaster and reinforced by a scrim coat which should extend over both sides of the seam as far as possible. The same procedure is followed to assemble the back caps on to the mother mould, starting at the top and gradually working down to the base. It is possible to join the sections of the mould together by squeezing them after each seam has been coated with a paste-like consistency of plaster. It is rather difficult to achieve maximum control by this method and if the mould is correctly designed it should rarely be necessary.

### Removing the mould from the cast

After the mould has been filled it should be left to properly cure for at least twenty-four hours before any attempt is made to remove the mould from the cast. A waste mould is removed by chipping away the plaster case from the cast. This is made much easier if the scrim coat and various fastenings are first removed. If a clay wash was used, these should pull away quite easily, but a little water is sometimes necessary to get this started. The bulk of the cast is removed by carefully chipping it away a little at a time. The soft soap should help it to break away easily and the yellow tinted coat acts as a warning that the surface of the cast is being approached.

The chipping is done using a blunt chisel and a light wooden mallet. I must emphasize that this procedure is not carving and no attempt should be made to cut the plaster away. The chisel is lightly tapped so that the vibration gradually breaks up the plaster and the separator causes it to fall away from the surface. The chisel should always be held at right angles to the mould to avoid the danger of accidentally scoring the surface of the cast.

When the main bulk of the mould has been removed small picking tools can be easily improvised to assist in removing small particles from the deeper areas of texture. Immediately after the mould is removed, the cast will not be very hard and the seam marks and any other imperfections can be fairly easily removed using a wooden tool or very fine abrasives. Any necessary patching or additions to the sculpture can be modelled in plaster provided the cast is thoroughly clean and well soaked in water. The plaster cast can then be treated as the final sculpture and finished in one of the ways described in chapter 13 or, if a stronger sculpture is desired, it can be used as the master model from which a vinamould is taken.

10

# Making a vinamould

## The adaptability of vinamould

The waste mould method of casting described in chapter 8 is only suitable when a single model of the original sculpture is required. A vinamould provides the means for a series of copies and can also be used when it is necessary to take a mould from a sculpture already existing in a permanent material. The main reason for having more than one copy of the model is the accepted sculptural tradition of selling work in limited editions. This is done to spread the total cost over a stated number of pieces and so enable the sculptor to charge an economic price. A reproduction mould also enables the artist to be much more adventurous in his experiments if he is going to work with a material such as polyester resin, which can be treated in a great variety of ways.

Like so many of the processes involved in sculpture, the method of making a vinamould might at first sight appear to be rather complex. In fact, if the various stages are undertaken with care and patience, it should not prove too difficult even for the inexperienced sculptor. A controlled means of heating the vinamould and a special thermometer to check the temperature of the melted liquid are the only additions which must be added to the sculptor's basic range. The design and the making of the mould are very similar to those used for the traditional gelatine mould in bronze casting.

Vinamoulds can be taken from models made in a wide variety of materials, including almost all the ones commonly associated with sculpture. Wax is the only exception, because it would be melted by the heat of the liquid vinamould. It is possible to take a vinamould directly from an original clay sculpture but it is much safer to work with a material which is not so easily damaged and so it is usual to first translate the clay into a stronger material, using the waste mould method previously described. This is then known as the master cast and it enables the process to be repeated should any mistakes occur.

If the vinamould is to be taken from a non-porous material, such as polyester resin, the model will not need any special preparation, although it must be absolutely clean. With fragile glass or pottery objects where there is a danger that they might crack if subjected to sudden heat, it is best to warm them before pouring the vinamould.

If the mould is to be taken from a porous material, such as plaster or cement, the model must be either saturated with water or effectively sealed to prevent air bubbles from spoiling the mould surface. If there is any danger that the heat of the vinamould could turn the water into steam it is advisable to seal rather than soak the model. This is usually done by the application of a series of coats of shellac well diluted in methylated spirits. The shellac mixture should be brushed thinly over the sculpture and allowed to dry between coats. Thick shellac will not make a very good seal and by lying on the surface will tend to obscure the clarity of the original modelling. The effectiveness of the seal can be easily tested by the use of a few drops of water, which should remain on the surface if sufficient coats of shellac have been used. If more convenient, a suitable brand of resin-based lacquer can be used as a substitute for the shellac mixture.

A wooden model is difficult to cast in a vinamould, but if the object is not very valuable it can be treated in the same way as any other porous material provided the wood is heated to a fairly high temperature before the sealer is applied. If this might cause the wood to crack it can be sealed by applying a thin coat of catalized resin; however, once applied this cannot be removed and should not be used on antiques or other valuables.

### Casting the vinamould in sections

Vinamould is sufficiently flexible to enable most sculptures to be cast in one or two pieces but with large or awkward shapes the mould can be divided into any number of sections for ease of handling. The method of casting each section will be the same as that described for the first piece. It is necessary to make a separate plaster case for each section of the mould except when casting a very small sculpture or one in low relief. This case serves the dual purpose of controlling the thickness of the vinamould and holding it rigid when it is in use. The plaster must be designed so that it can be easily pulled away from the model, which means that the inside curve must never be greater than a half sphere. With this in mind a line should be drawn on the original model to determine the division of the mould. If possible, the model should then be laid down so that the section to be cast first is face upwards. It can be wedged with pieces of wood to improve its stability before a bed of clay is built up to the predetermined division line. This should project from the model, so that a seam of at least one-inch width is left, following the contours of the sculpture.

To help in relocating the pieces of the mould during the various stages, a series of spoon-shaped keys are at this stage added to the seam. The exposed half of the model is then carefully covered with clay, the thickness of which will eventually determine the thickness of the vinamould. It should be in the region of three-eighths to three-quarters of an inch depending on the size of the work being cast. Uneven thickness can cause distortion and so it is advisable to build up to the required thickness by using uniform coils of clay which allow maximum control.

A truncated cone of clay, which will become the pouring vent, is the next addition to the design. It must be sufficiently high to allow a good drop during the pouring and should be positioned over the lowest point so that the melted vinamould can flow over the model without any air being trapped in the hollows. Similar cones made so that they reach a uniform height are placed on the high points of the sculpture; these will become vents which allow the air to escape as the vinamould is poured.

The design is completed by the addition of a clay coil which is pressed so that it lies just above the seam line and again follows the contours of the sculpture. This will form a ridge which can be supplemented by clay studs and will eventually help to keep the vinamould in its case.

We have now covered a section of the sculpture with a clay replica of the proposed vinamould. The case is made by taking a plaster mould of this clay covering, using the method described for a waste mould but omitting the colour in the first mix and using the reinforcing scrim coat without the addition of a clay wash. The completed case is then released, to allow the clay to be removed, leaving a space, the exact shape of the desired vinamould, between the case and the model. The case is then sealed with shellac and reapplied, so that the melted vinamould can be poured through the appropriate vent into the designed space. It is possible to melt very small quantities of vinamould in an ordinary aluminium

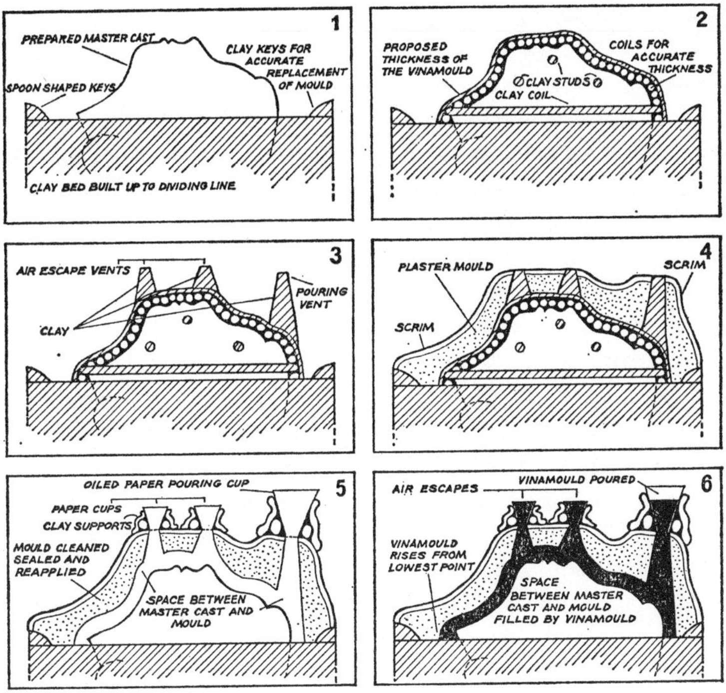


Figure 25 Diagram of the stages in making a vinamould

saucepan over a gas or electric ring. The bottom of the saucepan must be protected by an asbestos mat and the vinamould melted a few pieces at a time, constantly stirring to prevent it from sticking and burning.

If this method of mould-making is to be used at all regularly, however, it is worthwhile making an air bath, which is both easier to use and suitable for larger quantities. An air bath works on a similar principle to that of a double saucepan or glue pot but, as the melting point of all grades of vinamould is higher than that of boiling water, the heat must be allowed to circulate freely between the outer jacket and the smaller container holding the vinamould. Very large quantities are better melted in a specially designed thermostatically controlled melting pot.

The working temperatures of this medium are very precise and it is necessary to use a special thermometer to check that the correct melting and pouring temperatures have been reached. These readings must be taken directly from the liquid and the thermometer must not be allowed to come into contact with the container. When the correct temperature has been reached, the vinamould should be poured in a steady, even stream, as quickly as possible. If the material cools before the pouring is completed, it will be necessary to re-melt the whole amount and pour again. The size of each piece of a mould must not be greater than the melting capacity will allow to be poured comfortably. As a rough guide to the design of the mould size, one pound of vinamould is approximately twenty-seven cubic inches.

The completed section should be allowed to cool for several hours, preferably overnight, before the vinamould is removed from the model or the second section prepared for casting. The design of the case and the provision of pouring and air vents is done for the second and subsequent pieces in exactly the same way as previously described, except that the case of the first piece is used instead of the original clay bed. The hollow keys on the rim of the first case will act as position markers to ensure a true register when the pieces are finally assembled. Providing the second pouring of the vinamould is not at a higher temperature than the first the two sections will not stick together, but it is usual to dust the first piece with french chalk before the second one is poured. With more than two-piece moulds, clay walls are used to divide the sculpture into the required number of pieces. Completed moulds should be stored in a cool place and protected from grease and dirt.

## The grades of vinamould

Red vinamould, which melts at a temperature between 130° and 140°C and should be poured at a temperature of 120°C, is a medium-hard compound which allows a considerable amount of undercutting. It is particularly suitable for casts in plaster and can be used for polyester resin, if a long production run is not required.

Yellow vinamould is used at the same temperature as the red but it is much harder and is only suitable for sculptures with simple open forms.

Blue vinamould is melted and poured at 150°C. It is very soft and flexible and is usually used to produce small, intricate pieces in plaster or cement.

Green vinamould, which melts at 130°C and is poured at 120°C, is a flexible compound which is ideal for use with polyester resin.

Brown vinamould, which is melted and poured at 170°C, is a slightly harder version of the green. It is again suitable for use with most materials, including polyester resin.

Provided vinamould has been used at the correct melting and pouring temperature it can be cut up and re-used. If it is overheated it will lose its flexibility and will eventually crack. If it is allowed to burn it will become quite useless as well as causing one of the most unpleasant smells it has been my misfortune to encounter.

11

# Cement, polyester resin, and bronze

## Casting in different materials

We have seen in previous chapters the desirability of transferring the clay sculpture into a more permanent material. This chapter deals with the most popular materials used for this purpose.

Apart from the traditional plaster cast already described a mixture of cement and a variety of aggregates is one of the most common methods of casting. For very little extra cost in terms of time and materials it is possible to produce a finished sculpture which has considerable natural character with a reasonable degree of strength and durability.

Another material which is becoming increasingly popular with sculptors is polyester resin reinforced by fibre glass. This produces a cast which is even more durable and stronger than cement. It is also possible, with polyester resin, to use large quantities of decorative fillers; consequently the finished appearance of each cast can be chosen from a very wide range.

When metal powders are used as fillers, the sculpture is often described as being a cold metal cast. This is substantially true because up to 80 per cent of the material is actual powdered metal with the resin acting simply as a binder. The method of casting is slightly more complicated than with either plaster or cement, mainly because the material is difficult to handle and the mould needs careful preparation. It is also a little more expensive but the actual cost is largely determined by the choice of material used as a filler. It is probably better in the beginning to gain some experience of casting in general with either cement or plaster.

The most traditional and in general the best material for casting modelled sculpture is bronze. Even a slight acquaintance with the history of sculpture will serve to demonstrate the wide variety and subtlety of finish it is possible to achieve in this material. The fact that we can still enjoy so many of the works of antiquity speaks in itself for the durability of sculptures made in bronze. Unfortunately the cost of this process puts it out of the range of all but the wealthiest or most successful sculptors. This is not due to the actual cost of the metal but rather to the complexities of this casting process.

## Cement

All moulds must be designed and prepared for the material with which they are going to be used. With cement the only preparation necessary is to make sure that the plaster mould is clean and thoroughly saturated with water. This should be done by soaking the mould in a bath or casting sink, depending on its size. If for some reason this is not possible, the mould can be sealed with shellac and a wax polish used as an additional separator. Before starting to fill the mould, any surplus water or wax that might be lying on the surface must be removed. The design of a mould suitable for cement is very similar to that already described for casting in plaster, the main difference being that cement, unlike plaster, cannot be poured and so the design must allow access for filling by hand to all parts. The cement cast will be a different colour and density from the plaster mould and so there is no need for colour in the first mix used in making the mould.

Some sculptures are designed with the finished appearance of a particular cement in mind; *ciment fondu*, however, is the one most commonly used. It is a very fine grade black cement which is capable of reproducing the most delicate of modelled forms and can be finished to make an acceptable substitute for sculptures which would ideally be cast in bronze.

Cement on its own would not be strong enough for most sculptures and so it is only used without reinforcement for the first coat applied to the mould. This coat of pure cement is the one which takes the actual impression of the sculpture. The second and subsequent coats, which are known as the backing coats, are added to increase the stength of the cast, and for these the cement is reinforced by adding either fibre glass or sharp sand.

Both these materials have advantages and disadvantages. Fibre glass is comparatively easy to handle and produces a very light sculpture, but the backing coat has a tendency to separate from the pure cement coat, which makes it unsuitable for sculptures which may be subjected to extremes of temperature. A generally stronger but much heavier cast results from using a mixture of cement and sharp sand and I would recommend this for any large sculpture or for one which is to be exhibited in the open air.

For both methods the first coat is mixed and applied to the prepared mould in the same way. Before using the cement, if it has been stored for any length of time or if it is slightly lumpy, it should be sifted dry through a medium-fine mesh. Badly stored or damp cement will feel to be full of small hard particles when it is rubbed through the fingers. This should not be used for sculptures as it might lead to the loss of important detail.

After sifting the cement, the first coat is prepared by

gradually adding water to the dry powder, until it reaches a consistency when it is marginally more of a liquid than a solid. If necessary, more dry cement can be added to correct the consistency, which must then be mixed until there are no lumps of undissolved powder.

If the backing coat is to be made with fibre glass, cement and water are first mixed to a consistency which is more of a solid than a liquid. When correct, this mixture should retain its shape after being squeezed in the palm of the hand. If it crumbles a little, more water can be added, or more dry cement if the mixture is too liquid. It is again important that this mix is free from lumps and that it is of an even consistency. Loosely shredded chopped strand fibre glass mat is then added in a proportion of three parts prepared cement to one part fibre glass.

When the backing coat is to be reinforced by sharp sand, the two materials should be mixed dry in the proportion of one part cement to three parts sand before the water is added to achieve the same consistency as described for the previous backing coat. *Ciment fondu* does not have a very rapid curing rate and so it is possible to prepare sufficient quantities of the chosen mixes, to allow uninterrupted filling of the mould, for up to two hours. Both mixtures should be stirred regularly while they are in use and any mixture not actually in use should be covered with a damp cloth.

The cement is applied to the mould by liberally coating a small area at a time with the pure cement mixture which is then reinforced by pressing small quantities of the second mixture firmly into place to build up the backing coat. Care must be taken at this stage that the filling is not allowed to project over the edge of the mould, as this would prevent the cast from being reassembled correctly at a later stage. For the same reason, the seams must be thoroughly cleaned before the cement is left to harden.

The thickness of the cast will vary with the size of the sculpture, but as a rough guide I would suggest that a life-size portrait head should not be less than half an inch if fibre glass is used, or one inch if the cement is mixed with sand.

Extra strengthening can be given to the fibre glass backing by pressing large thin sheets of glass fibre mat into the backing coat, after it has been pressed into the mould but before it has hardened. With both methods it is usual to reinforce thin or projecting parts of the sculpture with prepared square section mild steel rods, which are used in the same way as that described in an earlier chapter on casting in plaster.

After each separate part of the mould has been filled it should be covered with a damp cloth and polythene before it is left overnight to harden, in a cool damp place. Under no circumstances should any attempt be made to reassemble the pieces of the mould until the cement in each has been allowed to harden properly.

Similar mixes to the ones used in filling the mould are used to join the pieces together and the method used is the same as the one recommended for large plaster casts. Once again the separate pieces must be thoroughly soaked before they are joined together. The filled mould should be allowed to cure properly for at least twenty-four hours before the cast can be chipped out in the traditional manner. With cement this process is less nerve racking because the cast should be much stronger than the plaster mould. Carelessness or impatience at this stage, however, can still be dangerous. The unavoidable seam marks and any other imperfections can be removed by using small files and pieces of carborundum. It is very important that any work done on the cement cast is sensitive to the form of the sculpture because it is very difficult, in this medium, to disguise careless file marks.

One other method of casting in cement, which I would like to include because of its decorative quality, involves the use of selected marble chippings as the reinforcing aggregate. Unfortunately, this method is only suitable for sculptures which have been specifically designed to be completed by this method. using large open forms and a minimum of texture.

The mould is designed as usual for cement casting but only one mix is used in the filling. This is made up of three parts coloured marble chippings to one part of cement mixed with water, to the same consistency as the backing coats previously described. The absence of the first pure cement coat means that the cast surface will be irregular, with a number of holes, but this is unavoidable if the decorative pieces of marble are to be clearly seen. After curing, the cast must be thoroughly soaked before these holes are filled, using a putty-like mixture of cement. When these surface repairs have in turn been allowed to cure, a polished surface which shows the marble to

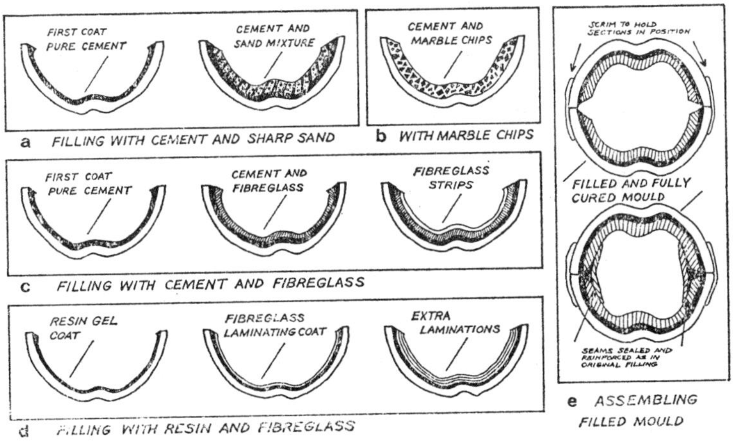


Figure 26 Diagram showing the use of different casting materials

advantage can be achieved by patiently rubbing down the whole cast, using first a carborundum stone, followed by carborundum powder, then pumice powder, and finally a light wax polish.

## Polyester resin

When polyester resin is used as a casting material, proper storage must be organized because both the resin and the chemicals associated with its use are delicate and inflammable. They must not be allowed to come into contact with naked flame or exposed to high temperature. The catalyst, which is an organic peroxide, must be kept in a cool and well ventilated space. It must never be mixed directly with the accelerator as this could cause an explosion. All other materials should be stored in a dark place and kept at a temperature below 20°C (68°F), preferably in metal containers. Under these conditions they will have a shelf life of six months or more. Exposure to heat or bright sunlight can make some of these materials useless in a matter of days. I would for this reason advise the sculptor to buy only enough material for his immediate needs at any one time.

Casts in polyester resin and glass fibre laminate can be taken from a variety of moulds and formers. In sculpture, vinamoulds, plaster waste moulds and moulds made from resin and fibre glass are all commonly used. It is very important that each mould is treated with the correct separator, before the resin is applied, because polyester resin has a very high bonding strength and while curing will adhere to almost any surface. Vinamoulds do not need any special treatment providing the surface is completely dry and free from dust and grease. Resin moulds must be fully cured before any separators are applied. The surface is then polished with a special release agent wax and if colour is going to be used at any stage on the cast the polish is covered with an even coat of quick-drying polyvinyl alcohol. This type of mould is only suitable for sculptures with large open forms and a minimum of texture. The traditional plaster waste mould can be used with polyester resin but, being porous, it needs to be very carefully prepared. The mould must be first absolutely dry and then sealed with a series of coats, using either a diluted mixture of shellac or at least three coats of cellulose acetate. If the sculpture is not unduly textured, this can be followed by polishing with release agent wax and a final coat of quick-drying polyvinyl alcohol. In cases where the wax could cause loss of important detail, the sealing coat should be followed by a series of coats of concentrated polyvinyl alcohol diluted with four times its volume of water. This must be applied evenly, and twenty-four hours drying time allowed between coats. Regardless of which method is used to seal the mould, it should always be completely dry before the resin cast is started.

Most resins used in sculpture are supplied with accelerator already added and are activated by adding a fixed proportion of catalyst, according to the supplier's instructions. The resultant mix should have a pot life of about forty-five minutes at a room temperature of between 65°F and 70°F. To obtain a successful cure at temperatures below 65°F, or to increase the setting rate of the resin, further accelerator can be added but I would not recommend working with resin in temperatures below 50°F.

The first coat of activated resin applied to the prepared mould is known as the gel coat because it must be allowed to harden before the laminating coats of resin and fibre glass are added. The first coat is considered to have gelled when it feels slightly tacky to the touch but allows the fingers to come away clean. This gel coat, which takes the impression of the sculpture, can be mixed with metal powder, fillers and pigments to produce a wide variety of finishes. The addition of any of these will in some way affect the general behaviour of the resin and it is always advisable to carry out a series of tests before using them for the actual sculpture.

Metal powders should always be finely ground, after which they can be used in as large a proportion as four parts metal to one part resin. The effect of metals, except aluminium, is to retard the setting of the resin and when they are used extra accelerator must be added. A too rapid or too slow cure must be avoided and this can always be controlled by the amount of accelerator added. Metal powders, specially ground for use with polyester resin, are available in bronze, brass, copper, lead, nickel silver and aluminium. Bulk fillers, such as china clay, powdered quartz and asbestos flour, are commonly used in industry to reduce the overall cost of the casting.

In sculpture, fillers are used mainly for their decorative effect and tests should be carried out using any dry, finely powdered material, so that some individual finishes can be produced. Special pigments in a paste form can also be used in the gel coat. These co-polymer pastes are obtainable in British Standard colours of red, orange, green, blue, pale yellow, pale blue, turquoise, grey, black and white. They can be mixed together to produce a wide range of shades, but this must always be done before the paste is added to the resin, otherwise the cast may turn out unpleasantly streaky. The gel coat must always cover the mould as evenly as possible and should have a minimum thickness of at least one-eighth of an inch. On sculptures with a lot of texture, more than one gel coat can be used to achieve an even coating of the surface.

The cast is then reinforced with laminating coats, using approximately one and three-quarter pounds of resin to the square yard. The glass fibre laminate is achieved by lying strips of chopped strand mat on to the resin, allowing a two inch overlap. The fibre glass is then impregnated by pushing it down into the liquid resin, using a dabbing movement with a stiff short bristle brush.

To achieve maximum strength, it is important to make sure that no air is trapped between the gel coat and successive laminating coats. For most sculptures two or three coats are usually sufficient but with large flat forms extra reinforcement in the form of previously impregnated glass fibre rolls, can be incorporated to give added strength and rigidity. When using resin in hollow or steep-sided moulds, 10 per cent of thixotropic paste can be added to the mix to prevent the resin from flowing too freely and collecting in the hollows. As the thrixotropic paste will not include any accelerator, a little should be added at the same time as the paste. The ingredients must then be mixed thoroughly before the catalyst is added.

Each piece of the mould should be filled separately and allowed to cure overnight before reassembly. Once again great care must be taken not to allow the cast to project above the sides of the mould, which must be kept clean at all times. The method of assembly is very similar to that described for casts in other materials, the main difference being that with resin each piece must be kept absolutely dry. The joints are sealed with a mix, made exactly as the original gel coat and reinforced by glass fibre laminates.

After complete curing the cast should be left for twenty-four hours before the mould is removed. It should be left exposed to the air for a further twenty-four hours before any work is done to the surface. Seam marks and surface irregularities can again be removed by the use of files and abrasives. If metal powders have been used, the cast can be treated in the same way as ordinary metals, including the use of acids to obtain a patina.

When using resins it is advisable to protect the hands with a barrier cream and to make sure that the catalyst does not come into contact with the skin, as this could cause burns if not immediately washed in clean soapy water. If the catalyst should come into contact with the eyes, it can be very dangerous; they must be thoroughly washed with plain water and a doctor consulted immediately. During the casting process, resin can be removed from the hands using a proprietary cream. Before it has completely cured, resin can be removed from tools, brushes and utensils, with acetone or cellulose thinners. For ease of working, throwaway plastic or cardboard containers should be used whenever possible. All waste material which has been in contact with resin or curing agents should be disposed of regularly and not allowed to accumulate where they could become a fire risk. Providing these sensible precautions are taken, and a little patience is used in acquiring the necessary techniques, polyester resin is an ideal and versatile medium for the sculptor, which greatly extends his range for a minimum extra outlay in tools and materials.

### Bronze

Casting in bronze, the most traditional material for modelled sculpture, is a complex and expensive process, and in any but highly skilled hands can be dangerous. Although some artists cast their own work into bronze, it is more usual for this to be done in foundries which specialize in this type of work. I would like to conclude this chapter on materials with a brief outline of what this involves, so that the artist will have some idea of the process his work will undergo if he sends it to be completed in a foundry.

Most average sized sculptures are cast into bronze by what is known as the lost wax or *cire perdue* process. This is a method of great antiquity which has not radically changed throughout the history of sculpture. The first stage in the process is to transfer the clay model into a more permanent material to produce what is known as the master cast. This is usually done by the sculptor using the waste mould method. A gelatine or other flexible mould is then taken from the master cast, as previously described in chapter 9. Hot wax is then painted and poured into this flexible mould to produce a hollow wax cast of the original sculpture.

The thickness of the wax cast will determine the thickness of the final bronze and will vary, depending on the size of the sculpture, three-sixteenths of an inch being the minimum thickness for a life-sized portrait head. The hollow wax cast must be of a uniform thickness to prevent distortion and cracking, which could be caused by unequal shrinkage during the cooling of the metal. (Incidentally, the fact that metal shrinks prevents the production of unauthorized copies because a cast taken from an existing bronze will be significantly smaller than one taken from the original master cast.) The hollow wax cast is reinforced with a solid core made from a mixture of one part plaster to three parts grog (powdered fired clay or brick dust). Before the next stage in the process, the wax cast is secured to its core by projecting iron pins. At a later stage these will hold the core and the investment in their correct alignment.

The next stage is to design and make what is known as the pouring gate. This consists of a wax funnel and a series of rods which are attached to the wax model to act as runners and risers. They are placed so that the hot metal can flow easily through the runners to all parts of the mould, while the hot air and gases produced when the metal is poured can escape by means of the risers without damaging the final cast.

The prepared wax model and pouring gate are next completely encased in a fire-proof covering which is known as the investment. This is again made by carefully using a mixture of plaster and grog. The completed cast is then baked until it is red hot to melt away and totally remove any traces of the wax. The hot metal is finally poured into the space left by the melted wax, so that it reproduces the form of the original sculpture. This explains why the technique is known as the lost wax process.

Another casting technique is the traditional method of sand moulding for fine art. This, however, is an equally complicated and expensive process in which impressions are taken from the master cast by the use of a special casting sand. The design and the making of the mould, core and pouring gate in this difficult material calls for a high degree of craftsmanship and is rarely undertaken by the sculptor.

It is possible to use the less expensive industrial method of sand casting for some sculptures which do not make use of extensive undercutting. In this case, the master cast is normally cut up into pieces by the sculptor, which the factory then cast separately, producing a simple front and back cast for each piece. The sections are then either welded or bolted together. The final item, which adds to the expense of any of these processes, is the chasing which is necessary to remove the imperfections which are an unavoidable part of the casting. Fortunately, work originally cast in a less expensive material can be reproduced in bronze at a later stage. It is quite usual in exhibitions to see a sculpture described as 'plaster for bronze' which means that the work will only be cast into bronze if it is successfully sold.

12

# Terra cotta

## Clay and clay mixtures

The term *terra cotta* is derived from the Latin, meaning cooked earth. This is an accurate although primitive description of sculptures which have been baked in a kiln, in such a way that the impermanent nature of the clay has been changed. In general, terra cotta has become associated with the red-brown colour of clays with a high iron oxide content. It can, however, be usefully extended to cover all work where the techniques of the potter have been used in the production of sculpture. Examples of this gentle art are found in all cultures where sculpture is generally practised. The technique accommodates a vast range of styles, from the naïve requirements of the earliest civilizations to the sophistications of the Renaissance.

Most clays generally used in sculpture are suitable for terra cotta but the judicious choice of clay can produce a series of exciting variations in the final appearance. I have found that there is an extra satisfaction in working in local clays, which as well as producing some individual finishes, also help the sculptor to develop a sympathetic relationship with his material. Regardless of the type of clay used, it must be absolutely clean because the presence of any foreign matter could result in disaster when the work is fired.

When used for terra cotta, it is most important for the clay to be of a uniform texture and density, and so it is further prepared, immediately before use, by a process known as wedging. The clay is first thoroughly kneaded and shaped into a rough rectangular block. This is then cut in half and rejoined by bringing down one piece vigorously on top of the other. The reformed block is then rotated in a quarter circle and the process repeated until the sculptor is confident that his material is in perfect condition.

There are a vast number of different clays and additives, which are more rightly the concern of the potter, but if the sculptor intends to specialize in this type of work he will be well advised to seek further information from both practising potters and books primarily intended for them.

## Firing techniques

The technique of firing in a kiln to produce the finished work imposes a series of definite limitations on the artist. The most important of these is that the sculpture must be a hollow form of an even thickness. There are a number of traditional techniques used in fulfilling this requirement which are easier for the beginner if the overall composition of the work is of a compact nature.

One popular method is to build up the sculpture in solid clay until all the main forms are established. The model is then cut in half with a sharp wire and both pieces hollowed out. The uniformity of the thickness of these hollow forms is more important than their relative size, which will vary with different sculptures. The two halves are rejoined, using a slip made from the same clay as a bonding agent. This should be fairly thick, to minimize any difference in consistency and to prevent the formation of small air pockets in the join. In this method the condition of the clay is very important in relation to the ease of the operation. The harder the clay the safer it will be to handle, but it will be impossible to join the pieces together successfully if the clay is too dry.

Only actual practice with this technique will determine the exact limits in which it is possible to work, but under no circumstances should the sculptor attempt to join pieces of clay which have dried to the stage where they have started to change colour. Special wire tools are available from most suppliers to assist in the hollowing out process, and the use of a damp cupboard, which allows the work to dry out slowly in a controlled humid atmosphere, will give the artist greater control over the condition of his work.

A further method of producing a hollow sculpture, which can be used on its own or in conjunction with the first, is to build up the form on a simple armature, covered with several layers of paper, which can be removed from the model as soon as the clay has started to harden. A modern variation of this method is to build up the sculpture on a previously carved block of polystyrene, which can be easily burnt away as soon as the clay is firm enough to support its own weight. The nature of polystyrene allows the clay to shrink slightly without the danger of cracking, and when burnt it reduces quickly to approximately one-fortieth of its original bulk. Terra cotta can also be built up on previously shaped hollow clay supports, using the traditional pottery technique of building with either slabs or coils of clay rolled to a uniform thickness.

Regardless of which technique is used in the making of a terra cotta, the clay must be bonded so that no air is trapped between each piece. Internal supports of clay buttresses and ribs must also be provided for any large forms which might be structurally weak. The drying out must be done slowly and naturally, in as even a temperature as possible, and the work must never be fired until it is completely dry. Fortunately, most clays change colour very obviously as they are drying, and after very little experience it is easy to tell when they are ready. With large sculptures, however, it is sometimes necessary to protect the outside with a damp cloth, so that the inside dries at the same rate.

Probably the most important single characteristic of terra cotta is the shrinkage that takes place both while the work is drying and during the firing in the kiln. With some clays, this can be as much as one part in ten and it is always significant enough to be clearly seen. It is this shrinkage which determines

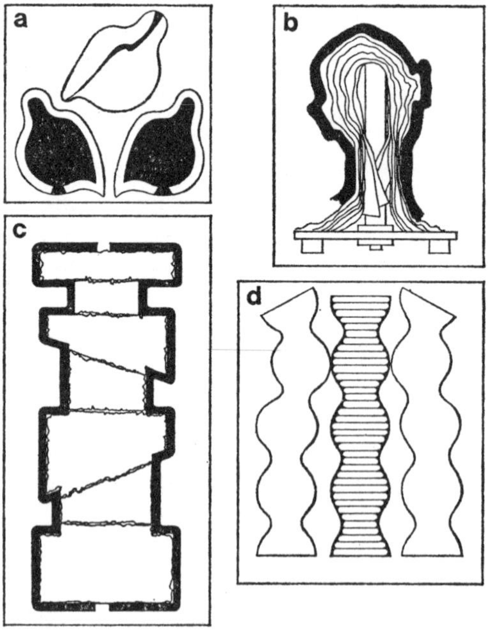


Figure 27 Diagram of some terra cotta techniques: a, solid clay form cut in half and hollowed; b, clay built up on a simple paper covered armature; c, clay built up on a shaped block of polystyrene; d, form built up on hollow clay coils

most of the technical requirements of the terra cotta techniques. Obviously, if the rate of shrinkage was uneven, due to lack of uniformity in the section of a sculpture, cracking would inevitably occur where the uneven areas met.

## The kiln

Firing is the descriptive name given to the process where by intense heat the chemical nature of the clay is changed into an insoluble material. This takes place at very high temperatures, varying from 1,000°C for earthenware to 1,250°C – 1,350°C for stoneware. To achieve these temperatures, and to control the speed at which they are reached, it is necessary to use a kiln which is specially designed for this purpose.

The most popular type of kiln used for sculpture is heated by a series of electrical elements, but kilns are also available fired by gas, oil, wood and coke. Only one firing is necessary unless the work is going to be glazed. In this first firing, the pieces of sculpture can be placed so that they are touching each other. Provision must also be made for the air to escape from inside the hollow form during the firing. A full kiln helps to spread the heat evenly and most kilns are equipped with a selection of fireproof stilts and shelves to assist in the economical packing of the work.

After packing, the kiln should be heated gradually, at first with the doors open, to make sure that everything is completely dry. The kiln should then be taken slowly up to the required temperature, held there for a little while so that the clay matures, and then allowed to cool slowly. It is very important that the cooling is not too rapid, and ideally it should take as long or longer than the firing. If necessary the doors, and any openings in the kiln, should be sealed to achieve this. The sculptor, like the potter, must control his natural impatience and never remove his work or even open the kiln doors until it is completely cold.

Some kilns are fitted with a pyrometer which records accurately the temperature inside the firing chamber but the traditional method is to use a series of special cones, packed into the kiln so that they can be clearly seen through a spy-hole. These cones melt and bend at predetermined temperatures and it is usual to use three, one just below the required temperature, one of the required temperature and one just above, for accuracy. Some very experienced workers can tell the temperature by the colour of the inside of the kiln, and while I would be reluctant to rely on this entirely, it is a skill which provides a useful extra safeguard once acquired.

## Glazing

Earthenware pottery has to be glazed if it is required to contain liquids, and although most sculptures do not have this requirement, glazes, used with discretion, can add a decorative quality to suitable pieces. This normally involves a second firing and if enamels are used a third or even a fourth. Most terra cotta sculptures are made in earthenware, but they can be fired up to stoneware temperatures if a suitable clay has been used. This increases the range of glazes and decorative techniques which the sculptor can use with advantage.

One of these techniques is to use a reduction atmosphere during part of the firing, which means burning any oxygen which remains in the kiln chamber. This can produce very dramatic effects, especially if metal oxides are used either in the glaze or in the clay body. The sculptor must remember, however, that at the high stoneware temperatures his work will be subject to considerable strain and even minor faults are likely to become apparent.

Firing even at lower temperatures will reveal any major weaknesses and terra cotta more than any other type of sculpture is likely to result in failure unless the craftsmanship is of a high order. The most dramatic of the possible disasters is when the kiln is opened to reveal only a heap of unrecognizable debris. This is usually caused by firing work which is not completely dry, but it can also be due to taking the temperature up too quickly. Allowing the kiln to cool too quickly will result in work seemingly intact but covered in small hairline cracks. This is usually due to damaged insulation, warped doors, etc. which are in turn due to a previous accident when the kiln was overfired, resulting in discoloured and misshapen work. If small areas of the work are shattered or if pieces have exploded away this will be due either to air bubbles trapped in the modelling or to the presence of some foreign matter in the clay body. The latter usually leaves a small discoloured area at the broken part. If cracks appear where the clay has been joined it means that either not sufficient or too thin a slip was used, or that the clay was too dry. Fine cracks which look rather like wrinkles are stress marks and they indicate that the clay has been treated rather brutally by bending it too often or by shaping it when it was no longer malleable.

In spite of, or perhaps because of, these difficulties terra cotta provides the sculptor with an unsurpassed range of natural colours and surfaces as well as enabling him to retain those delicate spontaneous touches which are a real part of the character of clay and which can often be lost during the involved casting processes of other methods.

13

# Carving in wood and stone

## The tradition of carving

The tradition of carving is almost as old as the human race; in fact, our knowledge of most early cultures is derived from the evidence provided by their sculptors. Today it is still practised in all societies, ranging from the technically advanced to the most primitive. It is perhaps significant that, because of the elemental nature of the relationship between the carver and his material, the most exciting and virile examples are not necessarily the product of the advanced cultures. The sculptor living in a technological society has one advantage, however, in that he can be aware of and influenced by the best work of all periods. A great number of famous modern artists openly acknowledge their debt to the anonymous craftsmen of more primitive societies.

The creative process, with its concern for observation, understanding and communication, which I have outlined in chapter 1, is appropriate to both carved and modelled sculpture. It is the method of manipulating the chosen material to the desired end which is radically different in the two disciplines. The essence of modelled sculpture is the gradual building up of the form, piece by piece, while the techniques of carving are exactly the reverse in that the unwanted material is gradually eliminated until the final form appears. The choice between modelling and carving will be determined by the personality of the sculptor and the requirements of a particular project. Once this choice has been made, the two important decisions which face the carver are how to remove the surplus material and how much material it will be necessary to remove. As one would imagine, with an art form of such great antiquity there are a number of well-tried traditional methods which can help the artist with both decisions.

## Carving in stone

Almost all stones, provided that their character is treated with respect, are suitable for carving. With the advantage of modern tools the actual hardness of a particular stone need not present too great a difficulty. It is important, however, to make sure that the chosen piece is free from flaws and is suitable for the intended sculpture. As a general rule, stone should be set up and carved so that its layers of stratification are lying in the horizontal plane. This will help to minimize the danger of cracking when the sculpture is exposed to the weather. The successful carver must be able to assess the likely behaviour of any stone with which he is likely to work and a general knowledge of the geological nature of his material, coupled with a study of how it has been treated by other artists, will be of great assistance to him. It is also important to gain actual experience by working directly with as many different varieties of stone as possible.

There are three basic groups of rock foundations, and the three most popular stones used in carving are each examples of one of these formations.

Granite, which along with basalt was used extensively in Egyptian sculpture, is an igneous rock, formed by the cooling of parts of the liquid subterranean mass. The exact quality of this stone depends on the depth at which this cooling took place. The colour is often variegated and ranges from black to pink. Speckled stone is often difficult to carve but the attractiveness of the finish often makes this worthwhile.

Limestone, which is part of the group known as sedimentary rocks, was formed by the gradual accumulation of layers of sediment. It contains a high proportion of calcium carbonate and is one of the easiest stones to work.

The stone originally favoured by the Hellenic sculptors, and which because of its natural beauty has always retained its favour, is marble. This is one of the stones found in the metamorphic group of rocks which result from the recrystallization, by extreme pressure and heat, of rocks from either of the other two groups. Once again there is a wide range of colour, which varies depending on the location of the deposit.

There are two traditional methods of removing the unwanted stone from the selected piece. Freshly quarried stone is ideal for either method of carving, but pieces of stone which have been exposed to the air for any length of time, such as pebbles, are likely to have a brittle outer covering and will probably crack if shaped by a hammer and chisel.

These stones are, however, suitable for the most traditional method of carving, where the surplus stone is removed by the use of abrasives. This method of making sculpture, by rubbing away the surplus material, originated before the introduction of specially tempered steel tools. If necessary, the surface can be pounded until it is sufficiently broken up to respond to the abrasive action of extremely hard stones such as carborundum. The considerable patience this lengthy process demands and the sensitivity of form which can result ensures the continuing popularity of this method. It is also used, in conjunction with a mallet and chisel, in the carving of very hard stones, when the surface has to be broken up before the chisel can gain a purchase. The technique has developed over the years. The

Egyptians used a dolomite pounder. The Greeks later used a metal chisel struck at right angles and bounced off the surface of their marble. Two modern tools are used today to serve the same purpose, the granite axe for very hard stones and the boucharde for the softer varieties.

On carvings where the bulk of the work is done with a mallet and chisel, a series of specialized tools are used in sequence. The first tool for carving a prepared block of stone is a pitcher. This should only be struck against a flat surface to remove large quantities of material. A point will then remove the rest of the stone up to about half an inch from the proposed surface. On a soft stone the form is then drawn more accurately with

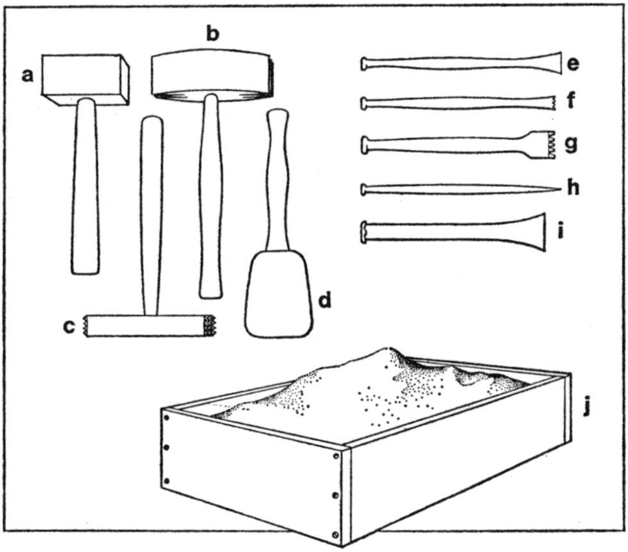


Figure 28 Basic stone carving tools: a, lump hammer; b, granite axe; c, boucharde; d, dummy mallet; e, chisel; f, claw tool; g, claw holder and bit; h, point; i, pitcher; j, sand box

a serrated tool known as a claw, while on harder stones the granite axe can be used to serve the same purpose. Chisels, which are available in a variety of sizes and are tempered to suit the type of stone being carved, are used to cut across the stone to produce the final surface, which can then be polished as desired.

It is important that all tools are maintained in good condition and they should be sharpened regularly during use. Slight variations in the design of carving tools are necessary because of the varied nature of different stones. In general, tools with a long point and a hard temper are suitable for marble, tools with a broad cutting edge and a hard temper are suitable for granite, and tools with a broad flat edge and a softer temper are used on the softer stones.

Useful additions to the basic equipment for sculptors are a special saw for cutting stone, a stone drill and special bits, a set of rifflers for use in abrading and polishing, and a sand box for holding small carvings while they are being worked. If large carvings are to be undertaken, the sculptor's studio must also be equipped with a special carver's banker, crowbars and blocks for lifting the stone, and a series of slings and pulleys so that the carving can be moved easily.

The actual designing of a stone carving can be approached in the same way as a wood carving, and so it will be possible to deal with them both together after I have described the techniques of carving in wood.

## Carving in wood

Each separate piece of wood, because of its organic nature, will have an individual character, but provided the artist has a sympathetic understanding, almost all woods are suitable for carving. As with other schools of sculpture, the most invaluable experience comes from actually working with as wide a range as possible. From the conifers we get the soft woods such as pine, larch and spruce, and from the deciduous trees such favourites as oak, mahogany and teak. In general, it is the type and figuration of the grain which determines the selection of a wood for a particular carving, wood with an open grain being suitable for large simple carvings, while the close grained woods, such as lime, apple and ebony, lend themselves to the carving of considerable detail.

Strictly speaking the wood used in carving is known as timber, and while this is not an important distinction the use of the correct term can help to establish a better relationship in the timber yard, which is actually the main source of the carver's raw material. The wood used in carving must be sound, that is free from cracks and well seasoned, and if possible the artist should check the condition of his selection before buying it. Good sound timber, if struck vigorously with a wooden mallet, will produce a loud clear ringing tone; a dull heavy sound would indicate the presence of water in the wood.

The process by which the natural water is allowed to dry out of newly felled timber is known as seasoning. On a commercial scale this is done in kilns which, by controlling the temperature and humidity, allow the natural drying process to be speeded up. Some of the most exciting woods, however, from the carver's point of view, have very little commercial value and are almost unobtainable ready prepared and seasoned. The serious carver is always on the look out for suitable timber and should try to make some space available for the seasoning of his finds. Raw timber should be roughly dressed and then stacked in such a way that the air can circulate freely around each log. Natural seasoning can be a lengthy process and, depending on the size and type of wood, can take anything from a few months to a number of years.

If the proposed carving will allow it, the drying time and the danger of cracking can be greatly reduced by boring a hole through the centre of the log and so increasing the area exposed to the air. Wood which has been previously used, such as timber salvaged from demolition sites or driftwood, will usually be already seasoned and should dry out fairly quickly. Driftwood etc. should be thoroughly washed before drying, so that later small particles of sand cannot ruin valuable tools.

To carve wood with control it is essential to use sharp tools and, if the wood is not properly secured, these can be dangerous. Carvings should never be held on the knee and the direction of the cutting must always be away from the body. There are a number of specially designed benches equipped with all sorts of delightful features, but for most carvers a good strong kitchen table, used with bench screws and G clamps, makes an acceptable substitute.

A traditional method of carving was to use a series of different sized adzes to bring the work gradually to a finish. This produces a very pleasant texture and can still be used with advantage on suitable sculptures, although today the adze or axe is usually used to rough out the bulk of the work, on fairly large carvings, before it is finally refined, using a series of gouges and chisels.

The choice of type and size of chisel, gouge and mallet will depend on the size and nature of the carving as well as on the sculptor's experience and strength of wrist. A sixteen-ounce beech or lignum vitae mallet and a one-quarter, half and three-quarter inch gouges with three slightly smaller chisels will provide the basic range, which can then be supplemented by more specialized tools as the need arises. The chisels and gouges should be fitted with round maple or ash handles. Mushroom shaped handles are not meant to be used with a mallet and are more suitable for the type of carving where the

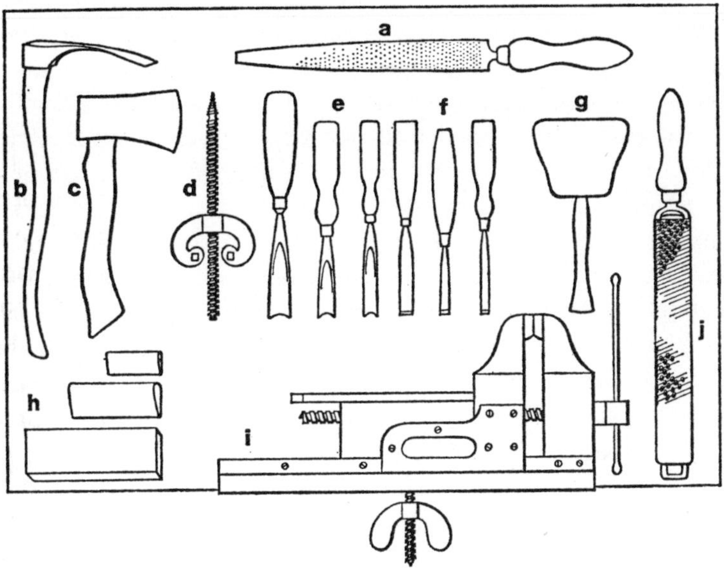


Figure 29 Basic wood carving tools: a, rasp; b, adze; c, axe; d, bench screw; e, three gouges; f, three chisels; g, mallet; h, slip stones; i, carrers' carvers' chops; j, surform

surplus wood is pared rather than chipped away.

Wood carving tools are delicate instruments which must be treated with care and regularly sharpened. This is a basic skill which is essential to all would-be carvers. It is also one of the first jobs that the beginner must learn to do because even new tools will need to be sharpened. A cutting edge of between 15° to 20° is ideal for soft woods, while an edge of between 20° to 25° is better for hard woods. The chisel, or gouge, is first sharpened to the required angle on a water-lubricated grindstone, which is easiest to use if treadle operated. The high speed of a power-operated wheel makes it too easy to overheat the tool, with subsequent loss of temper. A fine cutting edge is then given to the tool with the aid of one of the many varieties of oilstone, using a high-grade lubricant such as sewing machine oil. With gouges a rolling figure of eight motion is used so that the curved edge is sharpened evenly. Any fine burrs that remain on the cutting edge are then removed by slip stones before the final finish is imparted by the use of a buff hide strop. For safety the strop should be secured to a firmly fixed wooden block. Well sharpened tools, used correctly, will produce an excellent finish on most woods, but specially cut rifflers and paper backed abrasives can be employed to produce an exceptionally smooth finish if this is desired. Wood chippings collected during the progress of a carving can also be used in the final stages to fill up any cracks that might spoil the finish.

## Approach and design

If the potential carver can control his impatience, it would be very good practice to spend some time experimenting with the use of various tools in relation to the different materials. Then, as one acquires some skill and control of the tools, these experiments could be extended to cover a range of deliberate textures. Although time spent in this way might seem rather non-productive, the confidence gained will prove of lasting value.

The creative side of carving is very similar to that involved in other branches of sculpture, discussed in earlier chapters. The choice of material will to some extent influence the form of the subject but the intention of the artist will also influence the original choice of material. It is impossible to say that one sculpture is more suitable for carving than another. As a general guide, I would say that if a design would allow the natural quality of any material to be used with advantage, then that material would be suitable for that particular sculpture.

There are two main approaches to carving in either wood or stone. The first is popularly known as direct carving, which means that the artist makes the formal decisions about the shape of his sculpture while he is actually working on the final material. This has the virtue of involving the artist directly with his medium, but there is the disadvantage – especially for the inexperienced sculptor – that what started out as an ambitious mother and child can easily finish up as a rather insignificant torso, and although the artist should always feel free to modify his original design, he must also be aware of the dangers of self-deception if the final sculpture departs too radically from the original concept. In general, I think the direct method of carving is more suitable when the artist is working on a sculpture which has been suggested by the existing form of his material. The idea for a wood carving, for example, can often be suggested by the growth of a particular tree, and the natural formations of rocks and pebbles can influence the stone carver in the same way. The carving in these instances is a process of selection and refining to bring out and clarify a shape which is already inherent in the material.

The second method, in which the final design is arrived at by an experimental series of maquettes, culminating in a working model, is more suitable when the carving is to be made from a prepared block, especially if the artist finds this a non-emotive shape. Some artists prefer to carve this preparatory work from plaster, polystyrene or polyurethane, to retain a continuity of approach throughout the whole process.

There are a number of methods by which the working model, which must be to a definite scale, can be used to determine decisions about the final carving. The most precise of these involves a pointing machine, which enables accurate measurements to be related to both the model and the block of material. These measurements can then be transferred to the wood or stone, by boring holes to the same depth and then carving down to the point indicated. The disadvantage of this method of working is that it tends to be rather mechanical and prevents the artist from treating his material in a creative way. It can lead to the production of sculptures which are in no

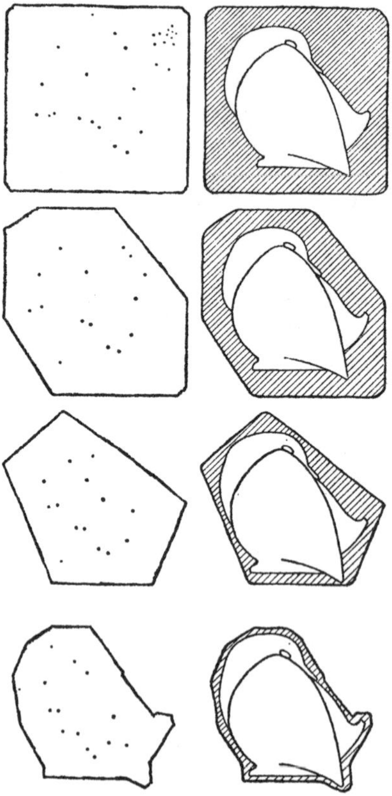

Figure 30 Diagram showing a plasticine covered model used to determine the stages in a carving

way sympathetic to the material in which they exist. As well as being undesirable to transfer work from one material into another without making at least some minor modifications, it is also difficult to change the scale of an idea without making some allowances for the different character of the final image.

A method of working which I have found very helpful is to use the working model as only a rough guide to the finished sculpture by using it mainly to determine the largest amounts of surplus material which can safely be removed at any one time. The model, which must be in a reasonably hard material, is first covered in plasticine so that it becomes a perfect replica of the block of wood or stone. As pieces of plasticine are then carved away from the model this shows that a similar amount of surplus material can be safely removed from the carving. By this method it is possible for the inexperienced sculptor to carve with some degree of confidence.

Once the broad outlines of a carving are established, the details can be worked out in relation to the real material of the sculpture. Regardless of which material or method the inexperienced carver chooses to develop, I would advise him to restrain his ambition in the early stages and to work on a sculpture where he has a reasonable chance of success. It is much better for his future development to produce a simple sculpture of which he can be proud, rather than to fail miserably at an ambitious carving of, say, 'The Last Supper' in marble.

14

# The finishing processes

## Some general hints

This final chapter deals with what is usually the most enjoyable aspect of sculpture, the finishing and exhibition of the completed work. Although patience is still needed, for what can be a fairly lengthy operation, the artist is at last dealing with a permanent and tangible object which exists only because of his previous labours.

Before dealing with the individual finishes associating with various materials, there are a few points which can apply to sculptures in general. The most important is to avoid highly polishing any sculpture which has not been designed with a shiny surface in mind. Over-emphasizing the highlights on any piece can cause apparent distortion and loss of subtlety. If a sculpture makes use of texture and dramatic undercutting the choice of a light colour or tone for the finish will enable the areas of light and dark to be clearly seen. On a sculpture where the form is much more important than the surface treatment, a darker finish is more desirable. Once again the study of other sculptures, and how they are finished and presented, will prove an invaluable guide.

## Finishing techniques

When plaster of paris is used as the final material, its appearance will be enhanced if it is first stained with a diluted solution of yellow indian ink, followed by a regular polishing with french chalk. This decorative finish, which looks rather like antique ivory, will reflect the light in a similar way to the original clay model and so result in a more faithful reproduction. A deliberate ivory-like finish can be given to plaster, once it is absolutely dry, by the repeated application of thin coats of skimmed milk until the surface polishes to a light sheen. When plaster is used for sculptures without any delicate surface modelling, it can be sealed with shellac and standard commercial paints then used with the appropriate undercoat.

Plaster casts are also the first stage in the bronze casting process and, because the work might not be transferred into metal until a much later date, there is a tradition of colouring the plaster to resemble the proposed bronze finish. The cast must be thoroughly dry before it is treated with a series of combined sealer and colouring coats. As the first stage, a variegated dark brown body colour is gradually built up, using finely ground raw umber, burnt umber and burnt sienna powder colour mixed with shellac well diluted in methylated spirits. To avoid blurring the modelling, the required density of colour should always be reached by using a series of thin coats. When the dark brown coats have been allowed to dry, and if a patina-like effect is desired, a further series of lighter green or blue-green coats are applied loosely so that they do not cover the whole of the surface. These lighter coats are made by mixing terra verte, veridian and cobalt blue again with diluted shellac. The colouring is completed by a further application of diluted shellac on to which bronze powder is dusted before the shellac has had time to dry. A cast treated in this way can look rather raw when first finished but an occasional polish with french chalk will eventually produce the required subtlety. Very slight variations in the colours used in the mixes will have a considerable effect on the final finish and so it is always worthwhile to make some tests on scrap plaster.

Ciment fondu, after casting in a plaster mould, is normally covered by a thin white bloom. This can be removed by rubbing it vigorously under running water with wire wool or a soft metal brush. Quite often, however, a judicious amount of bloom is left on the surface to give a subtle variation to the finish. On some sculptures a series of clear wax coats and a light polish is all the finish that is necessary. A most decorative variation of this method is to use a series of coloured coats made from diluted indian ink before the wax is applied.

Sculpture in cement which would ideally have been cast into bronze can be treated in the same way as previously described for a plaster cast. Very diluted coats of shellac must be used, however, because cement is not as porous as plaster and can easily take on a sticky appearance. A popular method of achieving a similar effect is to use the colour and the bronze powder in the same way but substituting a mixture of silicone wax and turpentine instead of the shellac and methylated spirits. This type of finish is particularly suitable if the colour need not be permanent.

Another easy and versatile method of colouring cement sculpture is to use acrylic based colours diluted with water to a dye-like consistency. These are applied to the cast when it is completely dry, and once the colours have hardened they become waterproof and very resilient. Except in special circumstances I would not recommend the use of colouring agents with the cement during the actual casting process. Under normal studio conditions it is very difficult to maintain a uniformity of colour throughout the numerous stages.

Polyester resin, when used with the standard colour pastes or bulk fillers, does not need any special treatment but it is sometimes necessary to remove traces of the separating agent by lightly rubbing the surface with acetone or a proprietary solvent. If the resin has been filled with metal powder, the cast will need considerable polishing to show this to its best advantage. The surface should first be cleaned by using a fine grade wire wool soaked in solvent, followed by a vigorous rubbing with dry wire wool, pumice powder, and finally metal polish. After this the cast can be treated in the same way as metal sculptures made by the more traditional methods.

In bronze casting, after the final mould has been removed, the first stage in the finishing process is to take off the runners and risers and any other imperfections from the completed cast. This highly skilled process is known traditionally as chasing. The raw areas left, after the pouring gate has been carefully sawn and carved away, are treated with matting tools and punches until the surface is indistinguishable from the original modelling. The whole cast can then be brought to a simple finish by the use of burnishing tools and very fine abrasives. Once a bronze sculpture is exposed to the atmosphere, the surface will tend to corrode and its colour can be radically changed. Antique sculptures which have been buried or left in the sea for long periods have what is known as a patina, the colours of which can be very beautiful. It is common practice for new sculpture to be treated with chemicals to produce artificially a similar finish. If this is to be successful, it is important to remember that the role of the colour is to enhance the form, which must be sensitively considered throughout the process.

The most common colours achieved by artificial patination are black, brown and a variety of greens. The basic chemicals used are ammonium sulphide and ammonium chloride, which must be diluted with water. They can be mixed with other chemicals to provide an almost infinite number of variations.

The chosen mixture is applied to the bronze by dabbing, pouring or brushing on to the surface of the cast which has been previously heated by a blow lamp. The final surface of all bronze sculptures should be protected with a lacquer or silicone wax coating.

The appearance of sculptures made in terra cotta is largely determined by the nature of the clay from which they were originally made and the temperature at which they were fired. The natural colours range from the palest of yellows through pink to a deep shade of purplish brown, but a sensitive borrowing from the art of the potter can extend this range almost indefinitely. If it is thought likely to improve the finish, unglazed terra cotta can be darkened and given a slight sheen by rubbing it with an inert oil, after it has been removed from the kiln but before it has completely cooled.

One great advantage enjoyed by the carver in wood or stone is that the major part of the creative work is done in a material which is naturally permanent. The aim of the finishing process in this case should be to enhance the character of the chosen material.

Stone can be finished by the progressive use of fine abrasives, followed by a clear wax polish. It is not possible or even desirable, however, to take all stones to a very high finish and so the original stone chosen for a sculpture must be sympathetic to the artist's intention. Because of the natural variations that occur, even in stones of a similar type, it is also important that the artist becomes sympathetic to his material once a particular stone has been chosen.

This dialogue between the artist and his material is also important in wood carving, where the natural textures resulting from the method of working can help to give character to the original intention. If desired a high degree of finish can again be achieved by the use of rifflers and fine abrasives. Most carvings, regardless of texture, are finally polished to protect the wood from damp and dirt and to reveal the natural colour and figuration of the grain. Any dirt or grease must always be removed by wiping the carving with a lint free rag soaked in methylated spirits.

A variety of methods can then be used, depending on the type of wood and the nature of the carving. The sheen produced by boiled linseed oil is suitable for most sculptures but this process takes a number of weeks to complete. The daily work involved however is comparatively light. For the first two weeks it is necessary regularly to brush the oil on to the surface, forcing it into the grain. The linseed oil is then slightly diluted with turpentine, to make it flow more easily, and the process continued until the carving is completely saturated. This will take about six weeks, if the mixture is applied daily. The carving is then allowed to dry and the final finish achieved by a regular and vigorous rubbing, using a series of dry lint free cloths.

Beeswax is another traditional and popular polish, suitable for most carvings. It must again be applied over a period of time, however, before the full beauty of the wood will be revealed. A high grade furniture polish containing beeswax can be used but most carvers prefer to make up their own paste. Natural beeswax is used for carvings in dark woods and the bleached variety for the lighter shades. The raw wax is coarsely grated into the smaller container of a double saucepan, and sufficient turpentine added to just cover the wax. The mixture is then gently heated over boiling water until the wax melts. The paste formed when it cools is then regularly rubbed into the grain and lightly polished when it is almost dry, This method can also be used to give a higher sheen to wood previously treated with linseed oil.

Soft woods are often sealed with shellac before wax polishing and shellac is also the main ingredient in french polish, which can be used on a carving if a very high gloss finish is desired. Most proprietary wood stains and dyes are imitative of other woods and I would not recommend their general use in carving, as the natural qualities of even the cheapest timber can be exploited by the sensitive artist. If colour is to be used, it should be employed wholeheartedly and the use of acrylics, diluted to a dye-like consistency, will make most of the traditional artist's colours available to the wood carver. Once these colours are thoroughly dry, the carving can be wax polished as desired.

## Mounting and display

Most sculptures are traditionally displayed mounted on a base or plinth. This needs to be carefully selected if the work is to be shown to its best advantage. It is quite often worthwhile to make a series of tests while the sculpture is still in clay, so that if necessary slight modifications can be made to the work at the same time as the proportions of the base are decided upon.

The main purpose of the base is to isolate the sculpture from its immediate environment and to provide a definite area of space for it to occupy. This will only be achieved if the base does not dominate or detract from the sculpture by being too large or too small. Each sculpture will present a separate problem and it is not possible to give any more specific advice than to say that a particular piece should always look to be perfectly comfortable on its individual base. Ebonized wood is a popular material used for this purpose. It is suitable for sculptures in different mediums because its uniquely reflective surface can occupy quite large areas of space without looking at all heavy. Its polished surface also picks up some of the colour of the sculpture and reflects it back towards the work so that one is always more aware of the sculpture than the base.

Some sculptors prefer to take advantage of the contrast gained by the deliberate use of a different material from the sculpture for the base. Exciting variations in colour and texture can be used in a similar manner. Plinths are often used in conjunction with bases to enable the work to be seen at the correct height, especially in non-permanent exhibitions. The modern taste is for these to be as non-obtrusive as possible.

When the work is finally finished and mounted, it is important for the artist to exhibit his sculpture to a wider audience and for him to see it in unaccustomed surroundings. In most areas there are local art societies who arrange a series of annual exhibitions and they are usually sympathetic to the inexperienced artist. After some practice it is possible to become more ambitious and to enter work for similar open exhibitions run on a national basis. The most famous of these in England is the Royal Academy summer exhibition, which has provided an opportunity for living artists to show their work for over two hundred years. Open exhibitions are now also organized by the Arts Council and similar bodies but I must warn the reader that because of the limited nature of the space available and the vast number of entries these exhibitions attract, much work of considerable merit has to be rejected. This unfortunate experience happens to all artists at some time and it must be met with persistence.

In addition to these non-profit making exhibitions there are also many commercial galleries devoted to buying and selling works of art. Once again these operate on a variety of levels, from the small provincial galleries up to the world-famous establishments of the London dealers. Most of the well-known galleries deal only in the work of established artists, with whom they have special contracts. They do, however, provide the public with the opportunity to see a much wider selection of contemporary work than would otherwise be possible. Provided the artist behaves in a reasonable, business-like way, most dealers are prepared to be helpful with advice and criticism. There are also galleries which are prepared to rent out space for exhibitions, as well as charging a commission on works sold. These must be treated with caution as it is possible that any money from sales will not fully cover the costs.

The opportunity to sell work is a natural outcome of exhibiting and this brings us to the problem of pricing a work of art. I would first advise against being too much influenced by the inflated prices paid for some pieces in the international salerooms. These works are considered primarily as investments rather than aesthetic objects and it is very rare for the sculpture of a living artist to reach this exalted status. On the other hand, I would not like to encourage the artist to undervalue his work.

If one is content to practice on a purely amateur basis, this attitude should be maintained also in relation to sales. Works disposed of as gifts avoid the unpleasantness of charging an uneconomic price and undercutting the professional artist, who often has to struggle to earn even a modest living. I find that the best way to arrive at a fair price is to calculate it on a time plus cost of material basis, and although it would be unfair to charge for time spent in acquiring the necessary skills, it is fair that the years spent in developing one's ability should be reflected in the price asked for a mature piece of work. As a conclusion, however, I must emphasize that by far the greatest reward for the artist lies in his own self-development and increased sense of awareness.

# Index